Where Have All the Voters Gone?

Where Have All the Voters Gone?

MARTIN P. WATTENBERG

HARVARD UNIVERSITY PRESS
Cambridge, Massachusetts
London, England
2002

Library of Congress Cataloging-in-Publication Data

Wattenberg, Martin P., 1956–
    Where have all the voters gone? / Martin P. Wattenberg.
p. cm.
Includes bibliographical references and index.
ISBN 0-674-00937-1 (cloth : alk. paper)—ISBN 0-674-00938-X
(paper : alk. paper)
1. Elections—United States.   2. Voting—United States.
3. Political parties—United States.   I. Title

JK1976 .W38 2002   2002024084
324.973—dc21

Contents

Preface

September 11, 2001, was election day in New York City. Thousands of New Yorkers will long remember that they were at a polling place to vote in the mayoral primary when they heard about the tragedy at the World Trade Center. For a time the contest was forgotten as people struggled to deal with the disaster. As preparations mounted for the rescheduled primary on September 25, the New York City Elections Board put up a large banner on its Web site reading "Vote. Or Liberty Is History." By all accounts, New Yorkers, like Americans everywhere, came to appreciate their liberties even more than usual in the shadow of September 11. But most apparently scoffed at the notion that their own personal participation in elections was necessary to preserve their treasured liberty. Only 13 percent of New York City's voting-age population turned out for the rescheduled primary. And when Michael Bloomberg won the race to succeed Rudy Giuliani by a slim margin in the general election, it was with the participation of just one-fourth of New Yorkers over the age of eighteen. This level of turnout was roughly equal to that of the previous mayoral election, but was substantially below the 34 percent turnout rate in 1993, when Giuliani was first elected. Furthermore, it was not just in New York City that the participation rates were disappointing. Two states held elections for governor in November 2001. Just 36 percent of the voting-age population voted in both New Jersey and Virginia (home to the damaged Pentagon). This rate of turnout was about the same as in the past two gubernatorial elections in Virginia, but in New Jersey it represented a significant downward shift in participation. Although polls showed that Americans felt more positively about their government after the terrorist attacks, such feelings had no positive impact on electoral participation rates.

There is nothing new about low election turnout in the United States. The last time the nation came to a halt and mourned for days on end—when John F. Kennedy was assassinated in 1963—this problem was squarely on the president's agenda. In fact, Kennedy had been scheduled to receive a presidential commission report on registration and voting participation on November 26, 1963, shortly after he was expected to return from Dallas. Looking at this report nearly four decades later, one is struck by the fact that virtually all of the commission's recommendations were eventually implemented. Commission members focused on ways to make it easier to register and to cast absentee ballots, and they could hardly have imagined just how greatly these procedures would be improved in the coming decades.

Nevertheless, turnout rates are much lower today than they were when this presidential commission made its recommendations. Registration reform, though well intentioned, just has not had an impact in terms of actually getting people to the polls. I am convinced that turnout rates in the United States would still be well below 1960s levels even if the country were to adopt the most efficient voter registration system imaginable. Efforts to get more people to the polls must look in other directions for solutions.

Yet in contrast to 1963, the problem of low turnout is scarcely on the American political agenda today. The controversy over the

2000 presidential election led politicians to concern themselves with the task of ensuring that citizens' choices are properly counted when they vote. The far more widespread problem of getting people to vote in the first place has not received serious consideration. This book argues that it definitely should.

The origins of this book date back to when I was completing my doctoral dissertation and my advisors pressed me to consider how diminished partisanship might have contributed to the decline in turnout. I am therefore indebted to them for stimulating my interest in this subject. As I worked on this topic, I enjoyed collaborating with Craig Brians, Ian McAllister, and Anthony Salvanto on specific aspects of voter turnout. They contributed to my thinking in numerous ways, and I owe them each a special debt of gratitude. Permission was kindly granted to reprint portions of the articles I worked on with these colleagues: Martin P. Wattenberg and Craig Leonard Brians, "Negative Campaign Advertising: Demobilizer or Mobilizer?" *American Political Science Review* 93 (1999): 891–899; and Martin P. Wattenberg, Ian McAllister, and Anthony Salvanto, "How Voting Is Like Taking an SAT Test: An Analysis of American Voter Rolloff," *American Politics Quarterly* 28 (2000): 234–250.

As this project evolved, numerous colleagues provided helpful comments and assistance in gathering data. I wish to especially thank Russell Dalton, Ivan Doherty, Mark Gray, David Farrell, Sibylle Hardmeier, Arend Lijphart, Matthew Shugart, Mark Steinmeyer, Aiji Tanaka, Ruy Teixeira, and Jack Vowles. The proliferation of Web sites made it possible to gather all sorts of tidbits of information and data that I could never have dreamed of a decade ago. More than any other single Web site, I found Klipsan Press's "Election Notes" (www.klipsan.com/elecnews.htm) to be invaluable in identifying articles about voter turnout.

My writings have been greatly improved by the hard work of

the Harvard University Press editorial staff over the last two decades. This project marks a change in the editorial supporting cast for me, and I am pleased to say that Michael Aronson and Elizabeth Gilbert have continued the tradition of excellent editorial work. I have heard from colleagues that many university presses no longer do much to improve an author's writing. That is certainly not the case with Harvard. Michael Aronson played an important role in directing this project, making many valuable substantive suggestions. Elizabeth Gilbert scrutinized every detail of the manuscript, improving the writing throughout and catching a number of oversights and errors. Any errors that may have made it into print are surely my responsibility.

Where Have All the Voters Gone?

Introduction

American elections are suffering from chronically low participation rates. In 2000, despite the fact that partisan control of the presidency, Senate, and House all appeared to be simultaneously up for grabs for the first time in generations, turnout was a mere 51 percent of the voting-age population. This followed a measly participation rate of just 49 percent in 1996, marking the first time that turnout in a presidential contest had fallen below the 50 percent mark since the early 1920s—when women had just received the franchise and had not yet begun to use it regularly.[1] In 1998 turnout in the elections for House seats was just 33 percent, even though many commentators painted this as a referendum on the Clinton impeachment debate. Young people, in particular, are passing up their opportunities to vote at alarming rates. According to U.S. Census Bureau studies, just 29 percent of eighteen- to twenty-year-olds voted in 2000 and only 14 percent participated in 1998. At a time when democracy is tentatively spreading around the world, America's low turnout rates provide a poor example for emerging democracies. If only a minority of people vote, and this group fails to be representative, then democracy suffers.

I believe that one basic aspect of U.S. politics explains much of why so few Americans vote as the twenty-first century begins: American elections are complex and anything but user friendly. This phenomenon is by no means new; throughout the twentieth century U.S. citizens were asked to vote for many offices (and frequently on referenda as well) at least twice a year in even-numbered years.[2] But two relatively new factors, weakened political parties and candidate-centered politics, make this high level of complexity ever more difficult to cope with—particularly for young people and citizens with below-average levels of education. When American political parties shaped the political environment they greatly simplified the voting process for most citizens; even those who did not identify with one party or the other could still benefit from a clear choice presented in starkly partisan terms. Thus political parties once provided the key glue that held the process together—getting people to the polls and simplifying a complex set of ballot decisions. As the political parties have declined in influence, so have participation rates.

The present state of American politics illustrates that sometimes there can be too much democracy. As Anthony King writes in a perceptive view of the American political scene from abroad, "the holding of elections in America has given birth to a major industry," an unusual feature of democratic life that he notes Americans take for granted.[3] In fact, only Switzerland rivals the United States among the world's established democracies in terms of the sheer amount of electing that regularly takes place. It is no mere coincidence that the lowest turnout rates, as well as the most demographically biased patterns of participation, are found in the two nations that ask their citizens to vote the most often and for the most items. The practice of democracy can indeed be taken too far, asking for more participation than many citizens care to dedicate themselves to. Rather than bemoaning how many Americans fail to exercise their democratic rights, we should be impressed with how many manage to vote in spite of a political system that asks more of a typical busy person than is reasonable. And rather than looking toward the ways in which advanced technology can further expand possibilities for democratic participation, we need to tackle the task of making elections more user friendly. Only then can we again realize the American ideal of widespread and egalitarian public participation in governance.

This book emphasizes what we can learn from an examination of the recent past, as well as the experience of other countries, in order to reverse the trend of declining turnout. My public policy suggestions focus on how American elections can be made more voter-friendly, such as by making election day a national holiday.

Historical and Scholarly Background

Throughout American history the trend has been to further democratize, opening up more and more avenues for public participation. The assumption has always been, with elections, that "if you build it they will come." By the 1840 campaign of "Tippecanoe and Tyler Too" the bold American experiment in democracy had proved to be a tremendous success. By then all White males had the right to vote—the widest level of enfranchisement ever known at that point in history—and 80 percent turned out. A generation later, Civil War soldiers on both sides regularly noted in their letters and diaries that they were fighting to preserve their concept of democracy.[4] We later entered two world wars in order to protect democratic ideals. Thus there is good reason to expect Americans to show up at the polls in accordance with their pro-democratic nature.

Until fairly recently most scholars expressed little worry about America's low turnout rates. *The American Voter,* which defined the field of voting behavior in 1960, devoted only about 5 percent of its attention to analyzing the choice of whether or not to vote.[5] This relative neglect of the turnout question seems under-standable in light of the fact that there was at that time still a good excuse for the comparatively low voter turnout in the United States—the aftermath of the Civil War. The states of the old Confederacy were long a major drag on the nation's turnout rate, owing to racial discrimination, the poll tax, and lack of party competition. By the early 1960s scholars such as Philip Converse foresaw an upswing in southern turnout rates due to ongoing urbanization of the region.[6] Furthermore, because turnout was found to increase with higher education, and educational levels were improving throughout the country, there was a clear expec-tation that turnout in the North would also rise.

Had scholars in the early 1960s been able to foresee other major societal, legal, and political developments, they would have been even more confident that America's turnout problem would be short-lived. The vast influx of women into jobs outside the home, if foreseen, would surely have led to an expectation of higher turnout, as women's lower turnout rate was attributed to their much lower level of participation in the workforce.[7] Furthermore, the civil rights movement of the 1960s led to developments that greatly spurred Black turnout rates to the point where they now scarcely fall below those of Whites.

The major unanticipated legal development over the last four decades has been the profound loosening of registration proce-dures. Registration hurdles have long been considered to be a central factor in keeping American turnout rates low. This was the case in the South, with its well-known provisions to prevent African Americans from voting, but also in much of the North—where the potential political power of immigrants threatened the early twentieth-century political establishment.[8] Raymond Wol-finger and Steven Rosenstone examined variation in 1972 state registration laws and estimated that if the most liberal of these had been in effect throughout the country, turnout would have been 9 percent greater.[9] Although registration is still the responsibility of the individual in the United States, since the National Voter Registration Act of 1993, commonly known as the "Motor Voter Act," was fully implemented in 1996 Wolfinger and Rosenstone's desire for liberal registration laws has been largely realized.

One of the reasons given for relatively low voter turnout in 1960 was the lack of perceived ideological difference between the presidential candidates. John F. Kennedy and Richard M. Nixon continued the usual pattern of the time, avoiding hard stands on most controversial policy issues, such as civil rights, and rarely making appeals through the liberal-conservative framework. Today, although one still frequently hears the charge that the candidates are too similar, the clear association that all Republican presidential candidates from Ronald Reagan to George W. Bush have made with conservatism has led to greater party polarization than existed four decades ago. In 1960, just 50 percent of the population thought there were important differences in what the two major parties stood for; by 2000, the same question found 67 percent seeing important differences.[10] We should naturally expect that turnout should go up as people see more distinction between the parties, all else being equal.

These reasons why turnout should have increased in recent decades all make perfect sense, creating a major paradox for scholars of voting behavior: despite expectations of higher turnout based on the societal and legal changes that have occurred, the national turnout rate has nevertheless plunged since 1960.

A Brief Look at Declining Turnout since 1960

Beginning this analysis of American voter turnout in 1960 might well be criticized as starting from an unnaturally high point. However, contrary to any notion that turnout that year was high strictly due to the excitement caused by the close Kennedy-Nixon contest, Converse and his colleagues wrote in 1961 that the increase in turnout had occurred mostly in the South.[11] And as Richard Brody showed in his now classic piece, "The Puzzle of Political Participation in America," if one graphs turnout rates from 1920 to 1960 there is a strong linear relationship, with an average increase of about 1.6 percent every four years.[12] Thus the relatively high turnout of 1960 represented not an anomaly, but rather the continuation of a well-established forty-year trend.

In the decades since 1960, the trend has been in the opposite direction, with a linear decline amounting to about 1.2 percent every four years.[13] The percentage of the voting-age population casting presidential ballots from 1960 to 2000 has declined as follows:

1960	62.8
1964	61.9
1968	60.9
1972	55.2
1976	53.5
1980	52.8
1984	53.3
1988	50.3
1992	55.1
1996	48.9
2000	51.2

Participation rates in midterm elections for choosing members of the House of Representatives have followed a virtually parallel course:

1962	45.4
1966	45.4

1970	43.5
1974	35.9
1978	34.9
1982	38.0
1986	33.5
1990	33.1
1994	37.4
1998	33.2

Turnout rates for other contests, such as primaries, municipal elections, and special elections are harder to come by, but these are typically abysmal, and I am not aware of any evidence that such rates have bucked the downward pattern in recent decades.[14]

It should be noted that all of the turnout percentages presented above are based on the voting-age population as the denominator, which includes noncitizens, felons, and other individuals who are not actually eligible to vote due to a variety of state laws. Samuel Popkin and Michael MacDonald argue that turnout decline is "largely an illusion," because the voting-age population has increasingly contained more people ineligible to vote because of rising immigration and crime rates.[15] Although these authors have a reasonable point, adjusting the voting-age population for noncitizens does not greatly change the pattern since 1960. When noncitizens are removed from the calculations, one finds that only about 54 percent of American adult citizens turned out to vote in 2000, as opposed to 64 percent forty years earlier.[16] This decline has been particularly pronounced outside the South, where the turnout of citizens declined from 71 to 55 percent between these two elections. It is hard to fathom how a change of this magnitude can be seen as illusory by any stretch of the imagination. And taking into account changes in the percentage of the population that is disenfranchised due to felony convictions (currently about 1.6 percent) is scarcely likely to change the pattern noticeably either.

Substantively, it is my view that the fact that noncitizens and felons are not voting is of importance, and that such information should not be ignored by removing them from the national calculations. Most of these people pay taxes and potentially stand to benefit from government programs as well. Whether it is right or wrong to exclude them from voting is not self-evident, as demonstrated by the varying franchise rules that have been applied throughout U.S. political history and which currently are in place around the world.[17] In his final message to Congress, President Bill Clinton recommended restoring voting rights to felons after they have served their sentences, a proposal that was subsequently endorsed by the National Commission on Federal Election Reform.[18] On the citizenship question, many leaders in the Latino community believe that those who are on the road to becoming citizens should be allowed to vote.[19] And in any event, noncitizens are counted in the Census, which means that the apportionment of political districts includes them. (In fact, there are districts in the Los Angeles area where the majority of adults are resident aliens. These people are probably receiving de facto representation, even though they can't vote for the people who represent their interests.) In sum, we need to take into account that such people are not voting today, just as the fact that people who were effectively disenfranchised by Jim Crow laws was taken into account in 1960.

Another concern about turnout statistics raised by the 2000 election concerns the numerator. Not every state keeps track of the actual number of people who cast ballots. Thus the best one can do is count up the votes cast for the highest-level office. But as the nation learned during the 2000 Florida recount controversy, not everyone who votes has a presidential choice recorded, either because he or she fails to mark a choice or because of technical problems with the ballot. A national study by Caltech and MIT estimated that this percentage has been approximately 2.3 percent of all voters in recent years.[20] If this percentage had increased in recent decades, then turnout decline might be slightly exaggerated. However, in 1960 *The American Voter* estimated a virtually identical percentage of invalid votes for president.[21] Relatively new voting technologies, such as punch cards, are therefore not to blame for declining turnout rates.

An Overview

In short, the recent decline in turnout rates presents a challenge for students of voting behavior that could hardly have been dreamed of when this field of study was founded. The classic early studies of voting were primarily concerned with ascertaining whether citizens could make wise decisions enabling their preferences to be faithfully translated into public policy. In the early twenty-first century, scholars must confront the questions of why so few people vote and what low participation rates mean for democracy.

The first half of this book focuses on factors that influence turnout rates, presenting data on the kinds of countries, U.S. states, and individuals in the United States who vote at the highest rates. Chapter 1 examines why American turnout rates are so low compared with those of other advanced industrialized democracies, as well as why falling turnout has become a worldwide problem. Chapter 2, on trends in the U.S. states, then examines the state characteristics and conditions that are associated with the highest rates of turnout decline. Chapters 3 and 4 present individual-level analyses: the former looks at what can be learned from sociological, psychological, and economic theories; the latter focuses squarely on the changing patterns of age and turnout over time, which have led to an alarming generation gap in electoral participation. The book then turns to a couple of questions concerning the political significance of turnout. Chapter 5 addresses the question of whether biases in who turns out affect election outcomes, finding that they do indeed, contrary to some of the most widely cited literature on the subject. Chapter 6 examines a specific form of turnout bias that drew intense scrutiny during the controversy over the Florida count in 2000—that of incomplete ballots, generally known in the literature as rolloff. Although problems with voting equipment no doubt account for some invalid votes, most of voter rolloff stems from voters' lack of information needed to complete ballots that often resemble multiple-choice tests. Because the media is the source of most information that voters obtain, Chapter 7 examines its role in turnout, focusing mostly on debunking the claim that negative ads discourage political participation. The concluding chapter presents a variety of lessons from abroad that might be used to increase turnout in the United States. The idea of making election day a national holiday is recommended not because it is likely to be the most effective change, but rather because it seems to have the greatest chance for passage, and would be the easiest to implement.

A Worldwide Turnout Problem

It is widely recognized that the United States has one of the lowest turnout rates among the world's democracies. Much less well known, however, is that turnout decline is by no means just an American problem. Most established democracies have seen their level of participation in elections fall substantially in recent years. This chapter addresses why American turnout rates are so low in comparative perspective, as well as why declining electoral participation has become a widespread problem in established democracies. The importance of strong political parties in bringing voters to the polls is a common theme revealed through an examination of both questions. As has long been recognized in the study of politics, parties are essential in mobilizing voters; recent experience adds further confirmation to this long-held premise.

When E. E. Schattschneider wrote that "political parties created democracy" he was primarily referring to their historical role in expanding citizen participation.[1] In the era prior to the development of parties, voting was typically the purview of just a small percentage of the populace. Political parties both fought for an expansion of suffrage and mobilized the newly enfranchised to go to the polls. Conversely, throughout history when parties have failed to perform their functions, electoral participation has declined. The saga of electoral participation in advanced industrialized countries is thus one in which the state of political parties, and the party system more generally, has played a critical role. The United States presents an important case study of the relationship between party system development and electoral mobilization. The very first party system in the world appeared in the United States in the late eighteenth century, and historians generally credit the emergence of parties with significantly increasing the levels of turnout. William Chambers writes that turnout figures from this period "show voting participation increasing as party development and rivalry advanced."[2] These nascent parties served to stir up interest in political questions and to provide a vehicle through which to channel popular participation.

Most of the leaders of America's first party system did not consider themselves professional politicians, however, and the idea of a regularized party opposition had not yet been conceptualized.[3] Party leaders who lost their bids for office often withdrew completely from the political arena rather than trying to mobilize voters for political change. The Federalists, in particular, were poorly organized, and by 1820, after repeated defeats, they no longer even bothered to offer up a presidential candidate. As this first party system crumbled, it is notable that turnout fell off dramatically—in many states by as much as half.[4]

The rise of professional politicians in America's second party system led to the development of party organizations as a means by which to regularly mobilize the electorate. The sharp rise in voting turnout from 27 percent of White adult males in the multifactional U.S. presidential election of 1824 to 80 percent in 1840 is often attributed to the development of keen nationwide party competition. Chambers writes, "A strong sense of identification with or loyalty to the party and its symbols, an attachment which had never developed in any significant measure in the first party system, became the order of the day."[5] Getting to the polls to support one's party came to be seen as a social duty to be performed regularly.

In sum, as Robert Dahl states in his classic study of politics in New Haven, "before the extensive development of political parties more or less in their modern form, voting turnout was sporadic."[6] Sometimes burning issues would get nearly half of the eligible electorate of New Haven out to vote, but other times the turnout could drop below 10 percent. The establishment of highly developed grassroots party organizations led to a great surge in turnout and a stabilization of participation rates, according to Dahl.

The American experience can be generalized to other democracies. As modernization proceeded in other countries that today make up the Organization for Economic Cooperation and Development (OECD), turnout increased hand in hand with the development of stable and well-organized political parties. Leon Epstein observes that "whenever a nation extended the right to vote to relatively large numbers, parties developed in evident response if they did not already exist."[7] Epstein further explains that the parties' function of regularized labeling became indispensable when candidates could no longer expect much of the electorate to know them personally and hence be able to assess their qualifications.

Bingham Powell's study of twenty-nine democracies in the 1960s and 1970s argues that modernization is associated with higher turnout because it leads to party systems that are firmly linked to demographic factors such as class, religion, and ethnic identity.[8] The fact that modern party systems reinforce social cleavages makes it possible to mobilize citizens on the basis of their group identifications. Powell maintains that in traditional premodern societies, in contrast, parties are often little more than coalitions of local notables that rely on personal appeals. His empirical analysis demonstrates that such premodern political systems have lower turnout rates than systems with modern political parties.[9]

The current American candidate-centered system harks back to premodern politics in some important ways that help explain why U.S. turnout rates in the high-tech age are among the lowest in the world. Furthermore, the trends in party politics throughout the advanced industrialized world indicate that other countries are becoming more like the United States than vice versa.[10] These trends have transformed parties in many countries into institutions that are less likely to be effective in getting voters to the polls than they once were. Low turnout remains a problem that is particularly acute in the United States, but there is now worldwide concern about falling levels of electoral participation.

Why the United States Ranks So Low on the Turnout Ladder

Supposedly a comment often heard in Arkansas when Bill Clinton took over as governor was "Thank goodness for Mississippi," because that state's dismal performance on economic and educational indicators could always be counted on to keep Arkansas from being ranked dead last. When it comes to turnout rates in established and/or populous democracies, perhaps Americans should say "Thank goodness for Switzerland," since otherwise their turnout rate would rank at the absolute bottom of the ladder. As can be seen in Table 1.1, only Switzerland has recently had lower turnout rates in terms of voting-age population (VAP) for major national elections to choose a government or chief executive.[11] The average turnout rate displayed in Table 1.1 is 72.1 percent, whereas the participation rate in the U.S. presidential election of 2000 was a mere 51.2 percent.

Why does the United States score so relatively low in terms of electoral participation? Five major factors have been widely discussed by scholars. Differences in registration procedures are the

Table 1.1   Recent turnout rates for established and/or populous
democracies

Country, year, and type of election	Turnout rate
Indonesia, 1997, parliamentary	92.8
Italy, 1996, parliamentary	87.4
Iceland, 1996, parliamentary	87.0
Israel, 1996, parliamentary and prime minister	84.7
Denmark, 1998, parliamentary	83.1
Belgium, 1999, parliamentary	82.6
Greece, 2000, parliamentary	82.0
Australia, 1998, parliamentary	81.9
Spain, 1996, parliamentary	80.6
Finland, 2000, presidential	79.4
Sweden, 1998, parliamentary	77.8
Brazil, 1998, presidential	77.2
Portugal, 1996, parliamentary	77.2
Norway, 1997, parliamentary	76.9
New Zealand, 1999, parliamentary	75.7
Germany, 1998, parliamentary	75.2
Austria, 1999, parliamentary	72.8
France, 1995, presidential	72.3
Netherlands, 1998, parliamentary	70.2
Russia, 1996, presidential	67.5
Ireland, 1997, parliamentary	66.7
Bangladesh, 1996, parliamentary	64.6
Japan, 2000, parliamentary	62.0
Mexico, 2000, presidential	60.0
India, 1999, parliamentary	59.7
United Kingdom, 2001, parliamentary	55.4
Canada, 2000, parliamentary	53.4
United States, 2000, presidential	51.2
Switzerland, 1999, parliamentary	34.9

Source: Calculated by the author based on data collected by the International
Institute for Democracy and Electoral Assistance.
   Note: Turnout rates are calculated from the percentage of the voting-age
population.

reason most frequently cited. Another possible explanation is the fact that America is one of the few major democracies that still votes during a workday. That American voters are limited to only two viable choices, which makes their party system unique among the world's major democracies, is a third major factor. As a corollary, the absence of a socialist party alternative is often seen as being responsible for the markedly poor turnout rates of America's lower classes, surely a contributing factor to low turnout overall. And finally, the extraordinary complexity of the American political system—a characteristic shared only with Switzerland among the established democracies—also probably inhibits voter turnout. Each of these factors will be discussed below.

It is frequently said of American voter registration that it places a greater burden on those seeking to vote than do the requirements of any other democracy. As David Glass, Peverill Squire, and Raymond Wolfinger categorically state, "The United States is the only country where the entire burden of registration falls on the individual rather than the government."[12] Roy Pierce challenges this assertion through a detailed comparison of registration procedures in France and the United States. Pierce estimates that as much as 19 percent of the age-eligible population in France is not registered, roughly equivalent to the current figure in the United States.[13] He concludes with the judgment that "it is more difficult to become a registered voter in France than in the United States, but once one is on the electoral roll a French citizen is less likely than a U.S. citizen to be removed from it and to face the need to reregister."[14]

In a variety of other countries, there is now good evidence that the electoral lists are not only incomplete but getting more so. The government of Canada formerly took the initiative to add all eligible voters to the electoral list, but today their procedures resemble those of the United States, in that it is up to individuals to complete the registration process.[15] The percentage of the VAP on the Canadian electoral list has fallen from 96 percent in 1953 to 85 percent in 2000. In New Zealand, voter registration is required by law, though penalties have never been enforced. In the 1999 New Zealand election, about 9 percent of the eligible voters were not registered, compared with just 1 percent in 1951.[16] In Great Britain, the *Economist Newspaper* reported that the percentage of people missing from the electoral register had nearly doubled over the last thirty years, because mobility rates have risen and because the poor have chosen not to register, to avoid first the poll tax and then the council tax.[17] Registration problems now even pop up in British fiction; the best-selling diaries of Bridget Jones contain the story of her unsuccessful struggle to vote on May 1, 1997, because she apparently ignored the registration form she received in the mail.[18] In a 2001 real-life attempt to get more people to return their registration forms, the Nottingham City Council offered a prize of one thousand pounds in a random drawing from among those who returned their form by a specified date.[19]

The recent turnout rates of these other countries that also have difficulties in getting all their citizens registered belie the notion that America's registration process is primarily responsible for its low turnout. These other nations, despite difficulties with registration, have all usually experienced substantially higher turnout rates than those found in the United States. Of course, if the governments of these countries were to take on the responsibility of registering all their citizens—as is the case throughout Scandinavia, for example—then no doubt turnout would be slightly higher in all of them. One can hardly argue with the notion that there must be at least a few people who do not go to the polls because they are not registered. It would certainly be desirable for all nations to have an efficient, reliable system for ensuring that all those who are eligible to vote are registered. But given the fairly good turnout rates in France and New Zealand, and in the

United Kingdom prior to 2001, it would seem more reasonable to conclude that most everyone who wants to vote can cope with the necessary procedures. The fact that these other countries, despite registration difficulties, typically have had turnout rates so much higher than the United States indicates that registration plays only a minimal role in deterring turnout.[20] (Additional evidence for this argument will be found in the next chapter.)

Probably a greater deterrent to electoral participation than registration is the fact that Americans must find time during a workday to vote, thereby preventing some people who might have intended to vote from doing so because of other commitments during the day. No new democracy that I am aware of has copied the American practice of voting in the middle of the week, and 70 percent of the established OECD-member democracies have chosen a weekend voting day in recent years. Indeed, Mark Franklin's careful multivariate analysis demonstrates that countries that vote on a weekend or holiday have a 6 percent higher turnout rate than would otherwise be expected.[21] A study by Jean Blondel and his colleagues of turnout in European parliamentary elections found that time factors accounted for 38 percent of circumstantial abstentions in countries that voted on a weekday compared with 19 percent in those that voted on Sunday.[22] Although these authors note that Sunday elections had a slight downside by increasing abstentions caused by people who were away from home, this would not be much of a factor in the United States, where postal balloting is well established for people who plan to be out of town.[23]

Besides having a convenient time to vote, turnout is also promoted by offering citizens a wide range of viable alternatives, thereby increasing the chances that one's vote will closely match one's political preferences. Most comparative studies of turnout have found that proportional representation (PR) tends to promote turnout, because it ensures that substantial voting blocs will be represented in government.[24] Furthermore, Powell points out that only the United States is "truly a two party system," because in other systems that are organized by single-seat districts competition is "usually between the equivalent of three parties."[25] It should be noted that these third parties in other non-PR systems are not limited to regional parties. The Liberal Party in the United Kingdom has long mounted challenges to districts throughout the nation, as has the New Democratic Party in Canada; in Australia, the Australian Democrats run everywhere against the two major parties under the slogan of "Keep the Bastards Honest"; and in New Zealand a robust five-party system had developed prior to the country's shift to proportional representation in order to make its parliament more representative of the votes cast.

In addition to limiting American voters to choosing between only two viable parties, the ideological spectrum is also uniquely narrow. Walter Dean Burnham has long argued that socialist parties elsewhere mobilize the working classes in a manner not seen in the American environment of competition between two middle-class parties.[26] Frances Fox Piven and Richard Cloward even go so far as to argue that the low U.S. turnout is due to intentional efforts on the part of early twentieth-century industrialists to keep the working classes from mobilizing, as occurred in most other democracies.[27] Whether intentional or not, the absence of a socialist alternative is exceptional among established democracies, and no doubt has contributed somewhat to lower American turnout over the years. It is worth pointing out that Canada, where the socialist New Democratic Party has never really been an alternative governing party at the federal level, currently also has one of the lowest turnout rates among established democracies.

Finally, it is perhaps most instructive to examine what the United States has in common with the one other established democracy with even lower turnout rates. This country is Switzer-

land, and the similarities it shares with the United States in terms
of the complexity of its political system and the lack of relevance
of its political parties may well account for the low turnout rates
in each. First, Switzerland, like many American states, regularly
employs referenda to decide specific policy issues that are left to
the parties to work out in most other countries.[28] Second, the
Swiss and American electoral systems are unusual among the established democracies in that they call upon their citizens to vote
for offices too numerous to list here. Third, Switzerland's Federal
Council is a unique executive branch that involves a form of per-
manent power sharing between the major parties on both the left
and the right—a system that is functionally equivalent to divided
party government in the United States.

All of these features add up to elections' being far more complex in the United States and Switzerland than in other established democracies. Political power is decentralized, thereby making it difficult for people to assess responsibility for governmental
performance. At the same time, Swiss and U.S. citizens are called
upon to make an incredible array of decisions at the polling
booth. In short, an examination of the American and Swiss cases
leads to the following proposition about turnout: build a user-
friendly electoral system and voters will come; build an overly
complex system and they'll stay away. In many ways, party politics in the advanced industrialized world has moved toward the
U.S.-Swiss model in recent years, thereby probably contributing
to the generalized decline in turnout rates.

Partisan Change in the Established Democracies

Scholars and pundits who write exclusively on American politics
often tend to assume that trends in U.S. political behavior are
caused by events unique to the United States. Vietnam and Wa-
tergate, for example, often get the blame for the rise of political

cynicism and the increase in the percentage of Independents, as well as turnout decline. But when one sees similar trends in a wide range of countries, then it is apparent that something systematic is going on and that the trend in any one country is not merely due to events specific to it.

In the case of turnout, numerous systemic reasons would lead us to expect a decline in electoral participation in established democracies—all of which have to do with changes in political parties. Virtually across the board it can be found that official party membership is down, as is party identification. Campaigns are now being conducted through television rather than through grassroots mobilization. Class-based politics has declined, whereas postmaterialist cleavages have arisen. Candidate-centered politics is no longer just the province of American politics, and the practice of shifting issues from partisan politics to direct referenda has also spread widely. All else being equal, these trends should lead to turnout decline in most established democracies.

Political parties organize for political campaigns just like generals organize for battle. Commanders raise an army for their campaigns; the functional equivalent for parties is its mass membership. Parties have traditionally relied upon their members to stand on the political front lines, carrying their message out to the electorate at large. Party members put up signs and pass out leaflets during the campaign. On election day, they work the phone banks and knock on doors to get out the vote. Taken together, these membership activities undoubtedly serve to stimulate turnout. Thus it is reasonable to hypothesize that the decline of party membership that Susan Scarrow, and Peter Mair and Ingrid van Biezen, report for most established democracies should lead to lower turnout as well.[29]

Even in the United States, where the practice of formal dues-paying members has never existed, grassroots organizations were prominent on the political scene for over a century. Such organizations quickly began to wither during the early years of television. Edward Banfield and James Wilson were among the first to note the impact of technology on parties when they ascribed to television the weakening of the importance of an American precinct captain's visits: "The precinct captain who visits in the evening interrupts a television program and must either stay and watch in silence or else excuse himself quickly and move on."[30] As voters throughout the world have come to experience campaigns through television rather than through personal contact with members of party organizations, voting has become less of a social act and more of a civic duty. Other types of social organizations could theoretically substitute for party organizations in mobilizing people to exercise their franchise. To do so, however, such organizations would need to become clearly politicized—a rare development in today's world. The net result is that fewer voters now go to the polls because they have been urged to do so by their friends, relatives, and neighbors.

The fact that party loyalty has generally declined throughout the OECD-member democracies, as shown by Russell Dalton and his colleagues, has set more potential voters adrift in a complicated political world without much-needed guidance to help them translate their opinions into voting actions.[31] Parties help to simplify the political world for the average citizen. Without this "user-friendly" method for making political choices, turnout should be expected to decline.

Even for those who continue to have an identification with a political party, there is reason to postulate that this identification is less likely to mobilize them than in the past. When partisanship was closely tied to class and religion, the association of social and political identifications provided a strong incentive for party identifiers to turn out. These linkages, however, have been considerably withered in recent years, as demonstrated by Franklin and his colleagues.[32] The logic laid out by Powell leads us to expect that as the bond between political parties and social groups declines, so should voter participation.[33]

The decline of class-based politics, in particular, has meant that traditional socialist workers' parties have been transformed. What Otto Kirchheimer termed the "catch-all" party has spread throughout most of the advanced industrialized world.[34] Most advanced industrialized party systems have seen a substantial lessening of ideological differences between the major political parties. Whereas going to the polls in many countries once involved choosing between a socialist and a nonsocialist government, today's partisan choices are rarely so stark. This long-term trend was accelerated by the discrediting of the socialist model when communism collapsed throughout Eastern Europe.

The weakening of social cleavages has also opened the way for the development of postmaterial cleavages in many advanced industrialized party systems. The rise of a new issue dimension would ordinarily be expected to stimulate turnout, because it would make party systems more relevant to current societal concerns. Postmaterialism, however, emphasizes the importance of political participation *outside* the political arena. Therefore, as Inglehart has noted, "In Postmodern society the emphasis is shifting from voting, to more active and issue-specific forms of mass participation."[35]

Whereas leftist postmaterialist parties have deliberately eschewed strong leadership, new parties on the right have emerged around charismatic personalities such as Jean Marie LePen in France, Joerg Haider in Austria, and Silvio Berlusconi in Italy. Although the personalization of electoral competition has appeared most prominently on the new right, it is a trend that is occurring widely throughout established democracies.[36] In a sense, the recent personalization of party politics harks back to the premodern factions to which Powell attributed the low turnout of lesser-developed democracies. As the basis for political mobilization, personalized politics is transitory and fragile, and is therefore another factor that should lead to turnout decline. Finally, the incentive for citizens to vote for elected officials has been lessened in many countries because of the extension of direct democracy. More referenda were held in Western Europe (excluding Switzerland, which has long practiced them) in the 1980s than in any previous decade, and this trend continued in the 1990s.[37] National referenda have included controversial topics such as membership in the European Union (various countries), divorce (Ireland), abortion (Italy), nuclear power (Austria), electoral reform (New Zealand and Italy), and whether to abolish the national army (Switzerland). When such issues are removed from the arena of party politics, the policy consequences of voting for national offices are lessened. For example, British turnout would probably not have fallen to new postwar lows in 1997 and 2001 had Labour been expected to make decisions on a common European currency, electoral reform, and Scottish and Welsh devolution rather than calling referenda on these subjects. Furthermore, by calling elections to settle policy matters that many people are not interested in, governments may be unwittingly fostering the notion that voting is not so important after all. Referenda such as whether to reduce the term of the French president in 2000 or Italy's 1997 vote on electoral reform referendum—both of which drew the participation of only 30 percent of registered voters—convey the message that democracy will survive just fine if many people stay home. Nonvoting can become a habit.

There is thus ample reason to hypothesize a generalized decline in turnout in the established democracies on the basis of recent changes involving parties in the electorate, parties as organizations, and parties in government. Perhaps the only aspect of recent partisan change that might be expected to stimulate turnout is the process of realignment that has been present in countries such as Italy, Japan, and Canada. The cyclical theories of Walter Burnham and Paul Beck posit that realignments make the party system more relevant to a new generation of voters and therefore stimulate turnout.[38] As will be seen near the end of this chapter, realignment has not served this purpose as of yet.

Demographic Factors and Turnout Change

In addition to realignment in some countries, there are various changes in the composition of electorates that might have been expected to lead to an increase in turnout in recent decades. Seymour Martin Lipset's 1960 classic entitled *Political Man* argued that "patterns of voting participation are strikingly the same in various countries." Among the patterns he noted were that "men vote more than women; the better educated, more than the less educated; urban residents, more than rural."[39] In the years since Lipset made these generalizations, these three variables have all changed in ways that should have led to higher turnouts, ceteris paribus.[40]

According to Lipset's summary of the then existent literature, women's lower turnout rate was due to the fact that so many were housewives. "The sheer demands on a housewife and mother mean that she has little opportunity or need to gain politically relevant experiences," wrote Lipset.[41] Since the early 1960s, however, there has been a vast influx of women into the workforce in advanced industrialized societies. Furthermore, issues specifically affecting women have entered the political arena, thereby politicizing many women who are not in the labor force. New value-laden gender issues such as abortion and equal rights have had an impact on all women, regardless of their employment status. Thus one no longer sees reference in the literature to a lower turnout rate for women. The development of gender equality with respect to participation in elections should therefore have served as a force increasing overall levels of turn-out since the 1950s.

Another revolutionary social change in recent decades has been the explosion of higher education. Contemporary electorates are the most educated in the long history of democracies. As Converse has stated, in analyzing "engagement in any of a variety of political activities from party work to vote turnout itself: education is everywhere the universal solvent, and the relationship is always in the same direction."[42] All else being equal, rising educational levels should contribute to increasing turnout rates in advanced industrialized democracies.

The third variable listed by Lipset, concerning the low turnout of rural voters, is hardly likely to be a factor reducing national participation rates today. Lipset wrote that the principal reason for this pattern was the social and political isolation of rural electorates. The development of television, however, has left scarcely anyone isolated from political news, and a much smaller percentage of people in advanced democracies now live in rural areas anyway.

Yet not every demographic factor that has long been known to be related to turnout around the world has changed in ways that spur higher electoral participation. The young have always had the lowest levels of participation, even in new democracies,[43] and most established democracies have expanded the franchise to eighteen- to twenty-year-olds since 1960. Married people have slightly higher turnout rates than the unmarried, and marriage rates have declined throughout advanced societies in recent decades. Union membership has fallen in most of these countries as well, a development that has reduced the stimulus for working people to vote.[44]

These changes in age composition, marriage rates, and union density, however, are scarcely as revolutionary—or as likely to affect turnout—as the boom in higher education, the movement toward gender equality, or the ending of the isolation of rural electorates. Overall, solely on the basis of demographic changes since 1960, electoral participation should be expected to show a generalized increase.

Evidence for Turnout Decline throughout the Established Democracies

The preceding sections raise a crucial question to be answered: which is more important in causing more or fewer people to go to the polls in established democracies, partisan or demographic changes? If the functions of parties are indeed critical to mobilizing voters, then it should be found that turnout has declined even in the face of largely countervailing demographic factors.

Table 1.2 compares the average turnout of the voting-age population in the first two elections of the 1960s with turnout in the two most recent elections in sixteen established OECD-member democracies. This selection of countries follows a scheme of analysis that compares similar systems. All of these countries have held elections continually since the end of World War II, populations of at least two million, and advanced industrialized economies. Australia and Belgium, which have both practiced compulsory election attendance throughout this period, are excluded from the analysis in order to eliminate an institutional variable that necessarily limits any noteworthy change in turnout rates. With the exception of the United States, the turnout percentages reported here are from elections for the lower house of the national parliament—for these contests usually decide who will form a government. The American electorate certainly believes that presidential elections are more important, as demonstrated by its higher participation rates in these contests. Thus an exception to the general rule is made for the United States by incorporating presidential turnout. Such an argument could also be made

Table 1.2   Change in turnout since the 1960s in established OECD-member democracies without compulsory voting (in percent)

	First two 1960s elections	Two most recent elections[a]	Percentage change
Switzerland	53.4	35.3	−33.9
Canada	74.2	54.8	−26.2
United States	62.4	50.1	−19.7
Netherlands	90.1	72.7	−19.3
Finland	85.3	69.3	−18.8
United Kingdom	74.5	62.4	−16.2
Austria	90.1	75.7	−16.0
Japan	70.0	61.2	−12.6
Germany	83.9	73.8	−12.0
France	66.0	60.6	−8.2
New Zealand	83.3	77.1	−7.4
Norway	81.4	75.7	−7.0
Italy	94.2	89.1	−5.4
Denmark	85.4	82.4	−3.5
Ireland	72.7	70.2	−3.4
Sweden	81.9	80.7	−1.5

Source: Calculated by the author from data collected by the International Institute for Democracy and Electoral Assistance.

Note: Turnout rates are calculated based on the percentage of the voting-age population. With the exception of the United States, where presidential elections are used, all elections are for the lower house of the legislature.

The Netherlands practiced compulsory voting in the 1960s, but abolished this requirement after the 1967 election. Italy has long had a compulsory voting law, but it has not been enforced.

a. As of June 2001.

for the semi-presidential systems of France and Finland. However, French citizens could only vote for president directly starting in 1965, and in Finland direct presidential elections did not begin until 1994.[45]

The results provide striking support for the conclusion that turnout has declined in established democracies. In all sixteen countries recent turnout figures have been lower than those of the early 1960s. It is rare within comparative politics to find a trend that is so widely generalizable. The mean change from the 1960s has been a 13.2 percent decline in turnout. To put this in perspective, these democracies currently have a total voting-age population of 581 million people. If recent turnout rates in these countries had been identical to those of the 1950s, an additional 52 million people would have voted—a number that exceeds the entire voting-age population of the United Kingdom.

Why has such a widespread trend throughout the world largely escaped notice whereas the American turnout problem has received much attention for decades? The answer is that the decline of turnout in established democracies aside from the United States is a fairly recent phenomenon. This can best be demonstrated by combining standardized data from these sixteen countries and plotting the year-by-year changes, as shown in Figure 1.1. For each country, the average turnout for the first two elections of the 1950s serves as a baseline from which to standardize all subsequent turnout figures. For example, if turnout had averaged 70 percent in 1952 and 1956 and then fell to 63 percent in 1960, the standardized turnout for 1960 would be 0.90. In order to smooth out the trends, a three-year moving average was calculated; therefore the data point for 1960 actually represents an average of all standardized turnout numbers from 1959 through 1961.

Figure 1.1 demonstrates that if there was any worldwide trend in turnout from 1960 through 1972 it was an upward one, as would have been expected from the demographic changes just outlined. It is only in the late 1980s that a clear decline in turnout in these countries, taken as a whole, can be seen. As late as 1989 the moving average had only once fallen as low as 0.95. After 1989, standardized turnout is consistently below the 0.95 level, and by 1996 had dipped to an all-time low of 0.84. In other

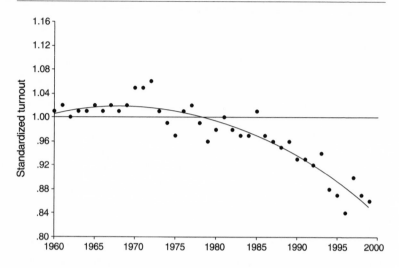

Figure 1.1 Turnout decline in OECD-member countries without compulsory voting in recent years. Entries represent a three-year moving average of standardized turnout numbers, with the average turnout in the first two elections of the 1950s serving as a baseline for each country. (Calculated by the author from data collected by the International Institute for Democracy and Electoral Assistance.)

words, turnout in these countries had been within a narrow band from the 1950s to the 1980s; the rapid decline of electoral participation is a phenomenon of the 1990s.

Such a pattern eliminates two possible explanations regarding the makeup of the voting-age population. It might be thought that the lowering of the voting age in most established democracies could account for much of this decline by enfranchising young people who are typically the least likely to vote. The decline in turnout in most countries, however, is found to occur substantially after this expansion of the franchise. Similarly, the increase in immigration could have lowered turnout based on the VAP by adding more noncitizens (who are typically ineligible to vote) to the denominator. The fact that turnout in established democracies declined so suddenly is incompatible with such an explanation. It is particularly noteworthy that the temporal sequence for turnout decline differs from that of the decline of party identification found by Russell Dalton in his examination of survey data from most of these same countries.[46] Whereas party identification has withered gradually, turnout decline as a general feature of advanced industrialized societies is primarily a recent phenomenon. This difference may simply reflect the fact that party identification is an attitude, whereas turnout is a behavior. It is common for mass attitudes to shift gradually over time, but it takes a major shock, or what Edward Carmines and James Stimson label a "punctuated equilibrium," to affect a habitual behavior like participation in elections.[47] There is little doubt that shake-ups in the party systems of the established democracies have provided the necessary jolt to send turnout plummeting.

An examination of the timing of turnout decline in the G7 nations will serve to illustrate this point, as a discussion of turnout decline in each of the sixteen nations would be unwieldy. In most of these G7 countries, it is possible to identify an election in which turnout fell more than 5 percent below the average for the first two 1950s elections and has never since risen back above this threshold. The commonalities in these elections are readily apparent. Turnout first began to decline markedly when the party systems of these countries experienced a major upheaval. Although the nature of partisan change differs, in each case the decline in the relevance of long-standing party cleavages—or of the major parties themselves—led to a smaller percentage of the population being mobilized to go to the polls. A chronological review of these critical points in the decline of turnout in the G7 nations will serve to flesh out this key point.

The first of the G7 countries to experience significant turnout decline was the United States, beginning in 1972. A portion of this decline was no doubt due to the expansion of the franchise to eighteen- to twenty-year-olds in that year. However, 1972 also marked a serious splintering of the Democratic Party. Arthur Miller and his colleagues noted that the majority Democratic Party was in "disarray," and hence unable to mobilize the electorate as effectively as before.[48] On the other side, Nixon won what many analysts termed a "lonely landslide" by running a candidate-centered campaign. The personalization of politics that was evident in this year marked the beginning of a sea change in American politics that resulted in a long-term dealignment.[49]

Other countries in the G7 did not begin to follow the U.S. pattern of declining turnout for quite some time. It was not until 1987 in West Germany that turnout decline was apparent for another of the largest democracies. This election marked the first campaign since the historic events of 1982–83, in which the Free Democrats' change of coalition partners led to a turn from a socialist to a nonsocialist government. After this shift had itself played out, the consequences of whether the Christian Democratic Union or Social Democratic Party held power probably seemed far less to many citizens, thus reducing incentives to vote in the future.

A very similar argument can be made for France, where the key date for turnout decline was 1988. In 1986, right-wing parties won control of the legislative assembly, thereby forcing President François Mitterrand, a socialist, into a power-sharing arrangement (cohabitation) for the first time in the Fifth Republic. After two years of cooperation between the left and right, fears of letting the other ideological tendance gain power could no longer be as effectively used by the parties to urge their supporters to go to the polls.

In the early 1990s, Canada, Japan, and Italy all crossed the threshold of noteworthy turnout decline as their traditional party systems collapsed. In Canada, the governing Progressive Conservative Party was reduced to a mere two seats in the country's momentous 1993 election. Despite the emergence of the Reform Party and the Bloc Quebeçois as new major players in the party system, turnout fell sharply and continued to slide downward in 1997 and 2000. Similarly, in Japan turnout dropped off dramatically in 1993 when the Liberal Democrats lost their majority for the first time since 1955 and the Socialists began to fade away. The development of various new parties, including one actually called "New Party," did little to spur turnout, and by 1996 Japanese turnout had hit a postwar low. In Italy, the corruption scandals of the early 1990s led to the disintegration of the governing Christian Democratic Party and to a reshaping of the left-wing parties as well. Candidate-centered politics emerged with full force in Silvio Berlusconi's Forza Italia in the 1994 election, which marked the key downward turning point for turnout in Italy.[50]

In contrast to the other G7 countries, the decline of turnout in the United Kingdom has proceeded in a zig-zag fashion, though the trend since 1950 is clearly downward, even if one excludes the precipitous drop in 2001 from the analysis ($p < .01$). It is noteworthy that the largest declines in participation took place after Tony Blair took over the Labour leadership and transformed it into a party much less tied to the union movement and socialist beliefs. Blair has repeatedly referred to the party as "New Labour." One cynical journalist asked him in 1997 whether he was going to officially change the party's name accordingly, or perhaps get rid of "Labour" entirely and call it the "New Party." Although easily laughed off by all at the press conference, this question nicely summed up the widely held view that Labour was no longer just the party of unions and the working class. As such a reconstituted party, it was far more successful in gaining a large vote share while at the same time less able to bring citizens of low socioeconomic status to the polls.

Significant shifts in party fortunes and the development of new parties have long been thought to be associated with increases in turnout. The fact that these partisan changes have occurred at the same time that turnout has plummeted in a number of countries suggests that dealignment rather than realignment is occurring. New parties appear to be appear to be less capable of mobilizing citizens than the parties of the past; the identifications with them are often based on short-term issues and hence are transitory. As Paul Abramson and his colleagues commented in 1998 about the United States, it is "difficult to consider any alignment as stable" when turnout is so low.[51]

Conclusion

Given that the decline of turnout in established democracies has been a relatively recent phenomenon, one can only speculate as to whether we are witnessing a long-term trend or merely a momentary aberration. Perhaps as new parties and patterns of competition become institutionalized, turnout rates will recover. But if turnout decline is indeed due to changes in the nature of political parties, then we can expect today's low voting rates to continue and possibly worsen. The candidate-centered mass media campaign is clearly here to stay, as are most of the other partisan changes this chapter has postulated as being responsible for declining turnout.

Parties, as organizations through which individuals seek office, unfortunately have little reason to be concerned about poor turnout levels. In fact, it is more efficient for a party to win an office with fewer votes. This would be akin to General Motors making just as much money with the sales of fewer cars.

Yet for the party system as a whole, lower turnout spells trouble, just as a decline in overall car sales would for auto manufacturers. In the political world, party leaders are the functional equivalent of CEOs, members of parliament function as upper-level management, and party members perform essential roles akin to those of assembly-line workers. On the other side of the supply and demand equation, party identifiers are like loyal customers, and those who vote represent the total consumer base for the product. If the CEOs, management, and workers of the auto companies were working more efficiently, but nevertheless selling fewer cars, industry analysts would no doubt conclude that the auto business was in dire straits. The fact that voter turnout has declined indicates that there is less of a market for the parties' product and that party systems around the advanced industrialized world have fallen upon hard times. Given that there is no one single cause for declining turnout, finding a solution that will work across the board (short of compulsory election attendance) will be difficult.

The fact that all established democracies are experiencing turnout decline might be seen as a reason for American policymakers to throw up their hands and say that if other countries are having the same problems then there is probably nothing that can work in the United States. Such pessimism would be mistaken. There are lessons the United States can learn from the experience of countries that have continuously maintained much higher turnout rates, and the Conclusion will return to these themes after more is established about the factors that account for whether Americans do or do not vote.

Turnout in the American States

The variation among American states in terms of turnout is nearly equal to the variation among nations. Some states have maintained relatively high turnout rates since 1960; others have seen far more rapid declines in participation than average; and most states in the deep South have seen turnout rates increase as discriminatory barriers to voting have been removed. Yet few comparative analyses of state turnouts have been conducted. Using aggregate state-level data from 1960 to 2000, this chapter seeks to demonstrate what can be learned from an examination of how states differ in electoral participation. What types of states currently have the highest turnout and why? Where has the decline of turnout been the greatest, and what accounts for the patterns that are found? Are differences in registration procedures really as important as the conventional wisdom would lead us to expect?

In past research, when variations between states have been included in analyses of turnout they have commonly been added to survey data as contextual data. Wolfinger and Rosenstone, for example, devote considerable attention to the role of state registration laws.[1] Their methodology involved taking Current Population Survey data and adding in entries for every respondent concerning that state's registration laws. By doing so they weighted populous states like California and Texas much more heavily than less populated states like North Dakota and New Hampshire. Thus the number of days one has to register before election day in California is put into a dataset of 80,000 cases approximately 10,000 times, whereas the same information for Wyoming is entered only about 200 times. Because of this method of weighting it is possible that a significant impact can be found when an independent variable has a positive effect in the four most populous states and no effect at all in the other forty-six. Similarly, Richard Boyd's analysis of how turnout has declined as states have separated their gubernatorial campaigns from presidential elections was based on an analysis of National Election Studies (NES) survey data, in which interviews are not even conducted in some of the states, and of course most people are from the more populous states.[2]

If what we want to know is whether particular state electoral procedures help or hinder turnout, then we do not want to set up a situation in which the vast majority of the variance in a dataset is accounted for by a handful of states with huge populations. Rather, the research design needs to be focused squarely on variation between individual states without regard to population size. In contrast to most previous research on the subject, therefore, this analysis will use each state as an individual observation.

State Variations in Turnout: 1996 to 2000

In the federal elections held between 1996 and 2000 there was a good deal of consistency in which states had the highest rates of participation among citizens. States like Minnesota, Maine, and Montana were consistently near the top of the list; others like South Carolina, Nevada, and West Virginia were consistently near the bottom. The correlation between state turnout rates in

1996 and 2000 was .88; the midterm turnout rate in 1998 had a
.64 correlation with both 1996 and 2000 turnout rates.

Unlike the turnout percentages employed in the previous chapter, the data on statewide turnout are calculated with noncitizens
excluded. Although there are no reliable estimates on the percentage of noncitizens for many countries, a reasonably accurate
estimate can be drawn for all American states by aggregating data
from the monthly Census Bureau studies. It is probably much
more important to make this adjustment for U.S. states, because
tremendous variation exists in the percentage of noncitizens. Sixteen states contained less than 2 percent noncitizens among their
voting-age population as of 2000, whereas this rate exceeded 10
percent in five states—with California topping the lot at 15.5 percent. California thus recorded a turnout rate of 44.1 percent
among its voting-age population in 2000, but among adult citizens its turnout was a more healthy 52.2 percent. Although it is
noteworthy to point out that the millions of adult noncitizens
who count in the apportionment numbers, pay taxes, and are eligible to receive government benefits are unable to vote, for the
purpose of identifying sources of variation in statewide turnout it
seems best to exclude them. (As far as I can ascertain, all previous
research using statewide aggregate data failed to make this adjustment to the data, and their findings may therefore be skewed by
differential rates of noncitizens over time.)

Table 2.1 displays the average citizen turnout rate for states in
1996, 1998, and 2000 according to various demographic, political, and legal factors. Probably the most common observation
about state turnout rates in the twentieth century was the distinction between South and non-South. As I noted in the Intro-
duction, this discrepancy has narrowed considerably over the last
four decades. Nevertheless, the South continues to lag noticeably
in terms of the turnout of its citizens. In each of the three elec-

Table 2.1 Mean state turnout rates of citizens in 1996–2000 by various factors (in percent)

	1996	1998	2000
Registration closes			
Election day	61.1	47.2	64.4
10–15 days before election	57.7	44.9	59.1
20–25 days before election	54.0	38.1	56.6
28–30 days before election	50.6	38.2	53.2
Congressional districts			
1	58.8	47.2	62.0
2–5	53.8	40.6	55.4
6–14	52.6	38.7	55.3
Over 15	52.7	39.1	55.0
Non-South	56.3	43.5	58.6
South	48.1	33.5	50.7
Education level			
Top third	57.2	43.2	60.9
Middle third	55.4	43.7	57.8
Lowest third	49.0	34.9	50.3
Per capita organizations			
Top third	58.7	47.7	61.6
Middle third	53.6	39.5	55.4
Lowest third	49.1	34.4	51.6
Contested and close races index			
0 to 1	50.9	36.4	55.0
2 to 3	54.8	43.4	55.2
4 to 6	52.5	37.2	59.5

Source: Calculated by the author from multiple sources.

tions from 1996 to 2000, southern states occupied at least seven of the ten bottom rungs on the turnout ladder. Georgia, Texas, Mississippi, Tennessee, and West Virginia were in the bottom ten every year. The highest any southern state ranked was seventeenth, which was Louisiana in 1996.

Besides the obvious barriers that were put up to discourage turnout in the South, another reason often given for the region's historically low turnout has been the lack of party competition. V. O. Key's classic study of southern politics in the 1940s even noted that primary turnout levels were frequently higher than in the general election, because the real contest for office took place within the Democratic Party.[3] Today the most lopsided presidential victory margins are found not in the South, but rather in New England on the Democratic side and in the nation's rural heartland on the Republican side. Yet many of these noncompetitive states have relatively high turnout rates, such as Massachusetts, Connecticut, Wyoming, and Nebraska. And on the other side of the coin, some very competitive states have consistently low turnout rates, such as Nevada, New Mexico, and Florida. In Table 2.1 states are classified according to an index of contested and close races for major offices in each year.[4] Interestingly, there is no consistent relationship between this index of competitiveness and turnout.

Such a finding, however, should not be taken to imply that turnout rates are completely unaffected by having more intense competition between the parties. States that become more competitive from year to year do usually see small improvements in turnout. For example, although turnout in Florida in 2000 was relatively low by national standards, it did mark a noteworthy rise for that state, and indeed caused some havoc with unexpectedly long lines at the polls. Curtis Gans found that turnout clearly increased more in comparison with 1996 in the so-called battleground states of 2000, whereas participation actually declined in many states the presidential candidates passed by, such as South Dakota.[5] But these are changes at the margin. It is unlikely that a low-turnout state like Arizona will suddenly move to near the top of the turnout ladder because of an intensely fought race, or that a high-turnout state like Wisconsin will see relatively low turnout if it moves into the noncompetitive column. In other words, there are enduring features of a state's political and demographic makeup that are good predictors of its typical turnout level.

One such aspect may be the relative size of a state's population. It seems reasonable to hypothesize that smaller states would have higher levels of turnout due to a more highly developed sense of community. In a small state, it may be easier for organizations to form and become capable of mobilizing friends and neighbors to vote. The local media are also more likely to focus on local politics in a small state like Montana than in a megastate like New York. In particular, in the major media markets of a state with a big population like California there are many congressional districts to cover, whereas this is not the case in places like Maine. Nevertheless the data display little evidence to support the theory that state population size is related to turnout rates. Only the seven states with just one congressional district stand out as having noticeably higher levels of voter participation.

Robert Putnam has proposed a more direct way of tapping community spiritedness through the concept of social capital. "The core idea of social capital theory," according to Putnam, "is that social networks have value." The concept "calls attention to the fact that civic virtue is most powerful when embedded in a dense network of reciprocal social relations."[6] As Steven Rosenstone and John Mark Hansen argue, people are more likely to vote when "someone encourages or inspires them to take part."[7] Thus states where many citizens are members of social organizations should have higher levels of turnout than states where individualism is more rampant. Fortunately, Putnam has provided state-wide data on organizational membership per capita on his Web site, enabling a test of this hypothesis.[8] Table 2.1 groups the states in thirds on this variable and shows that states with lots of social organizations do indeed have substantially higher turnout. It is noteworthy that organizational density seems to have an especially strong impact on turnout in a midterm election, when media attention to the campaign is less and group mobilization may well be even more important.

In addition to social capital, much previous research leads us to expect that educational capital should promote turnout. As Rosenstone and Hansen note, education gives "people the knowledge and skills that facilitate participation and [places] people in social networks that inform them about politics and reward political action."[9] Although much evidence has been established to demonstrate the impact of education on an individual level, the international patterns covered in the previous chapter indicate that there is not necessarily a relationship at the aggregate level. After all, the United States has one of the highest overall rates of educational achievement, yet has one of the highest percentages of nonvoters anywhere. But within the U.S. institutional context, it is clear that the states with the most educated populations do have the highest turnout rates. This relationship is not merely a product of the lower levels of education in the South; the pattern is quite evident in just the nonsouthern data.

Finally, it has long been recognized that states whose laws make it easier to vote have a higher turnout. Wolfinger and Rosenstone examined variation in 1972 state registration laws on three key dimensions: closing date, office hours for registration, and laws concerning absentee registration.[10] In their analysis of the effect of these state variations they argued that if the most liberal registration laws had been in effect throughout the country, turnout would have been 9 percent greater. Since the implementation of the Motor Voter Act in time for the 1996 election, the

only significant variation left in state registration laws is the closing date, which many argue is by far the most important.[11]
Wolfinger and Rosenstone noted that their 1972 data did not allow them to assess the impact of the most liberal of all registration laws—election-day registration.[12] Since 1972, Wisconsin,
Minnesota, Wyoming, Idaho, Maine, and New Hampshire have
adopted this procedure. In addition, North Dakota has no formal
registration at all, having abolished it in 1951.[13] As shown in Table 2.1, these seven states averaged very high levels of turnout in
each of the federal elections from 1996 to 2000.

Some evidence that would seem to support the notion that
election-day registration helps turnout comes from official data
posted on the Internet concerning when people actually registered to vote in two election-day registration states. In 1996, 15
percent of Minnesota's voters registered on election day, and in
Idaho the figure was 13 percent. Therefore, without the voters
who registered at the polls, these states would have had just
slightly better than average turnout rates. Of course many citizens in these states may simply wait till election day to register
because they know they can. Why register to vote a week or a
month ahead of time, if you can just take care of this on election
day? Richard Smolka's study of the adoption of election-day registration in Minnesota and Wisconsin found that many election-
day registrants were indeed procrastinators who needed to
change their place of registration.[14]

Given that registration laws are the most malleable of all the
variables related to turnout, it is no wonder that they have drawn
the most attention. It would be desirable, as Putnam argues, to
increase social capital, but this would take decades to actually accomplish. Similarly, most prominent politicians these days speak
about their aspirations and proposals to improve education in
America, but the effects of any policy changes will not be visible
for quite some time to come. But if a registration law is changed,
the effects are likely to be felt at the next general election. Thus

registration laws have become the favored target of reformers looking for a quick fix for America's low-turnout woes.

The Paradox of Easier Registration and Lower Turnout

The decline of turnout in the United States over the last four decades poses a paradox for students of political participation, because it has occurred simultaneously with a movement toward easier registration procedures. The 1965 Voting Rights Act made it possible for those who had faced discrimination in the past to register to vote, and the abolition of the poll tax removed any financial barriers to electoral participation. Federal law forbids states from closing the registration books more than 30 days before elections. And most recently the National Voter Registration Act of 1993 required states to permit people to register when they apply for or renew drivers' licenses (hence the name "Motor Voter Act"), and mandated that postal registration forms be made available at social service offices. All of these legal changes have facilitated the enrollment of more citizens than would have been the case without these laws. If one of the major reasons that so many Americans do not vote is that they are not registered, as has been frequently argued, then it stands to reason that turnout rates should have gone up substantially.

Yet, as shown in Table 2.2, the percentage of registered individuals who have actually shown up at the polls has generally declined. Over 80 percent of people on the registration rolls participated in the presidential elections of the 1960s; in 1996 less than two-thirds did so. The impact of more liberal registration laws, therefore, has apparently been to place more people on the rolls who then fail to vote. This pattern is particularly visible between 1992 and 1996. Although the Motor Voter Act led to large increases in registration rates in many states, the turnout rate of registered voters fell sharply—indicating that many of the new

Table 2.2 Percentage of persons registered actually voting, 1960–2000

1960	88.1
1964	83.4
1968	82.5
1972	74.5
1976	75.4
1980	74.3
1984	72.6
1988	70.5
1992	75.8
1996	64.3
2000	65.6

Source: Calculated using data made available by the Federal Election Commission. *Note:* From 1976 to 2000, the calculations are based on data from all states except Wisconsin and North Dakota, which do not maintain statewide registration lists. Data from earlier years are less complete, with 46 states being included in 1972, 44 in 1968, 40 in 1964, and 34 in 1960. However, in no case is data missing from a state larger than Missouri.

registrants did not make it to the polls in 1996. This can be demonstrated by examining changes at the state level: some states felt the impact of the new law more than others.[15] The correlation between the percentage of change a state experienced in registration from 1992 to 1996 and the change in the proportion of registered voters actually voting was −.81. This strong correlation provides clear evidence to support the theory that as the registration rolls swelled, the participation rate of those on them dropped.[16] Interestingly, the Census Bureau actually found fewer people saying they were registered in 1996 than in 1992.[17] The Motor Voter procedures apparently made registering so easy that many forgot that their names were on the voting ledgers.

Factors Influencing State Registration Closing Deadlines

In spite of these discouraging patterns, many scholars and political reformers concerned about low turnout rates continue to call for a further loosening of state registration requirements as a way of improving turnout rates. Particular attention is now turning to the closing date for registration. Even before the passage of the Motor Voter Act, Rosenstone and Hansen wrote that reformers had turned their attention to the wrong aspects of registration, ignoring the most important one—the closing date. They state: "Early closing dates, by requiring people to register long before campaigns have reached their climax and mobilization efforts have entered high gear, depress voter participation in American elections."[18]

In 2000, Senator Joseph Lieberman wrote that raising turnout rates should be "a hard national goal" and recommended that all states make it legal for voters to register at the polls on election day.[19] After the controversy over the 2000 election subsided, one of the first pieces of election reform legislation introduced in Congress in early 2001 was Representative Bill Luther's (D-Minn.) bill to mandate election-day registration throughout the country. No doubt these proposals will be criticized by conservatives as the misguided efforts of left-leaning politicians and academics to impose liberal laws on the states.

An examination of state registration laws in 2000, however, reveals that ideology has apparently played little role thus far in the establishment of varying states' registration closing dates. Of the seven states that allowed voters to register on election day or had no registration at all, Minnesota and Wisconsin are clearly on the liberal side of the policy liberalism index created by Robert Erickson and colleagues, Maine and New Hampshire are in the middle, and North Dakota, Wyoming, and Idaho are clearly on the conservative side.[20] Overall, there is an insignificant correlation of $-.08$ between policy liberalism and the number of days before the registration books are closed in a state.

Registration closing laws stem in large part from a state's political history and demographics, not its ideological leanings. Southern states had intentionally restrictive registration laws for many years, of course, and to many southern policymakers reducing the closing date to about the federally mandated minimum of thirty days was more than enough change. It should not be surprising to find that as of 2000 all but one of the fifteen southern states provided for voters to register at least twenty-four days in advance, the exception being Alabama, which set a closing date of just ten days prior to the election.

Another relevant aspect of political history is the former presence of traditional party organizations. Strong parties and partisanship are usually found to facilitate turnout, but an effective party machine is bound to focus on getting *its* people out to the polls. As the historian Alexander Keyssar writes, party machines "rapidly mastered techniques for insuring that their own voters were registered, and when in power, they often embraced the registration laws as a means of keeping other men and women from voting."[21] In particular, strong party organizations would not want to leave the door open to a last-minute mobilization of new voters. Although most party machines had withered away by the start of the twenty-first century, the impact of their historical presence can still be seen in registration laws. Of the thirteen states that David Mayhew classified as having strong party organizations in the 1960s, the mean closing-date cutoff for registration in 2000 was twenty-seven days, with Connecticut being the major outlier at fourteen days.[22] All of the election-day registration states were coded by Mayhew at the lowest point of his traditional party organization scale.

It must be remembered that registration laws were put into place to reduce voter fraud. Joseph Harris (later the inventor of the infamous punch-card voting system) wrote in his early study of voter registration that before such laws came into being "it was not unusual for armed men to appear at the polls and demand the right to vote," never to be seen again.[23] An amusing recent example comes from a Pennsylvania precinct in 1976, where it was recorded that Nikita Khrushchev, Richard Nixon, Gerald Ford, and Lyndon Johnson had all showed up to participate in the primary election.[24] Although not too many cases of voter fraud make the local television newscasts, they are crimes and people are occasionally prosecuted for them.[25]

Given their demographic differences, some states are likely to have less reason to be concerned about election fraud than others, and therefore to establish looser registration closing dates. In states where the crime rate is low it is to be expected that legislators would be more likely to take the chance of letting people register fraudulently at the last minute, when it would be hard to catch such crimes. Indeed, all of the election-day registration states recently ranked thirtieth or higher in the number of crimes per capita. Besides a relative lack of crime, a stable population should give policymakers less reason to worry about potential abuses inherent in last-minute registrations. If a high percentage of a state's citizens own their own homes, then registration officials are less likely to face such problems. Oregon, which currently ranks fortieth in terms of owner-occupied housing, became the only state to repeal an election-day registration law thus far after it experienced registration abuses by transients. As of 2000, the states with less than 65 percent of population in owner-occupied housing required a mean of eight extra days to register as compared with those that have higher percentages of home-ownership.

Table 2.3 summarizes the impact of all these factors by presenting a multiple regression equation predicting registration closing dates in 2000. All of the variables—South/non-South, traditional party organization score, crime rate, and percentage of the population living in owner-occupied housing—are found to be statistically significant in the predicted direction. An identical analysis (not shown here) using data from 1972 finds that these variables

Table 2.3   Predicting state registration closing dates in 2000

	Coefficient	Standard error	t-statistic
South/non-South (South = 1)	7.75	2.66	2.91**
State of party organizations in the 1960s (5 = strong; 1 = weak)	2.90	0.71	4.06***
Crime rate (per 1,000 population)	0.33	0.10	3.42**
Owner-occupied housing (in percent)	−0.53	0.25	−2.13*
Constant	31.88	18.67	1.71

***$p < .001$.   **$p < .01$.   *$p < .05$.
Multiple $R = .72$. $R^2 = .52$. $N = 50$.
Sources: Federal Election Commission (state closing dates); David R. Mayhew, *Placing Parties in American Politics* (Princeton: Princeton University Press, 1986), p. 196 (traditional party organization); *Statistical Abstract of the United States, 1999* (crime rate); *The Almanac of American Politics 2000* (owner-occupied housing).

explained only 47 percent of the variance, as opposed to 52 percent in 2000. Hence changes in registration closing dates since Wolfinger and Rosenstone did their classic analysis have been in the direction of what one would expect from state political history and demographics.

The Impact of Changing Registration Closing Dates over Time

Given that there is an inherent logic to the registration closing dates chosen by the states, one has to wonder whether stringent deadlines for registration lead to lower turnout or vice versa. Or perhaps there is really no dynamic causal relationship whatsoever, with other factors determining whether turnout rises or falls. A key question thus becomes whether states that have loosened their registration closing deadlines have seen less of a decline in turnout than other states. Since 1972, fourteen states have loosened up on their closing date by a week or more, whereas four states have tightened up their deadline by at least a week.[26] If one compares turnout in 1972 with turnout in 1996 and 2000, one finds that states that made registration more difficult experienced about 3 percent higher rates of turnout decline than states that loosened registration deadlines during this period. Although in the expected direction, this is not the sort of overwhelming impact that previous research would lead one to expect. Furthermore, there was no noticeable difference in trends between states where registration had become easier compared with those states where the closing deadlines had remained virtually the same.[27]

Yet another way of assessing the importance of registration laws over time is to examine whether states that currently have the most lenient deadlines have insulated themselves at least partially from the national pattern of declining turnout. Table 2.4 arrays the states according to their level of turnout change from 1960 to 1996—the presidential elections with the highest and lowest recent levels of participation. The states with election-day registration, or no registration at all, are italicized so they can easily be spotted. Some of these states, such as Maine and Minnesota, have indeed seen relatively little turnout decline compared with other nonsouthern states. Others, however, such as Idaho, New Hampshire, and North Dakota, are among those where turnout has fallen most precipitously. Most notably, presidential election turnout in North Dakota has declined from 79 to 57 percent in spite of the fact that it has had no registration requirements.

Analyzing Turnout Decline in the States

These state-level data demonstrate just how serious the waning of turnout is in some parts of the United States, including some of the states that make it easiest to register. Declines of over 20 percentage points are found in ten states, and another twenty-three states have experienced declines of at least 10 percentage points.

Table 2.4 Percentage point change in turnout rates among citizens from 1960 to 1996 by state

West Virginia	−32.8	Washington	−16.1	Montana	−7.6
Indiana	−27.2	New Jersey	−15.8	*Maine*	−7.1
Utah	−26.1	New York	−15.5	Hawaii	−6.2
Illinois	−24.5	Nevada	−15.0	North Carolina	−5.9
North Dakota	−22.2	Colorado	−14.7	Tennessee	−2.4
Delaware	−22.1	*Wisconsin*	−14.5	Arizona	−1.7
Rhode Island	−21.8	Vermont	−14.2	Florida	+4.3
New Hampshire	−21.3	Nebraska	−13.4	Texas	+4.3
Pennsylvania	−21.1	*Wyoming*	−13.2	Arkansas	+7.1
Idaho	−20.2	New Mexico	−12.9	South Carolina	+11.2
Connecticut	−18.6	Oklahoma	−12.9	Louisiana	+12.9
Massachusetts	−18.4	California	−12.7	Alaska	+14.0
Iowa	−17.4	Oregon	−12.2	Georgia	+14.4
Michigan	−17.3	Kansas	−11.8	Virginia	+16.3
Missouri	−17.1	*Minnesota*	−11.0	Alabama	+17.5
Ohio	−16.4	Kentucky	−10.1	Mississippi	+20.8
South Dakota	−16.2	Maryland	−7.8		

Note and Sources: Calculated on the basis of election results, U.S. Census estimates of the voting-age population in each state, and various Census data on citizenship. For 1996, citizenship rates for each state were ascertained by combining Current Population Survey data from September, October, and November of that year. For 1960, citizenship rates were calculated by adjusting Census data on the percentage of foreign born in each state using an estimate of 74% of foreign-born residents then being citizens. The estimate of the foreign-born population who were citizens in 1960 is based on an average of 1950 and 1970 numbers, as 1960 data were unavailable. States with election-day registration or no registration as of 1996 are in italics.

Those who believe that the decline of turnout is overblown due to the increase in noncitizens should note that these numbers reflect citizens only.

Where have the steepest declines occurred? Besides being primarily nonsouthern, the one aspect shared by most of the states with the sharpest dropoffs in participation is that they once had strong traditional party organizations. For the thirteen states that

Mayhew classified as high (4 or 5) on his party organization scale, the average decline in turnout was a staggering 19.3 percent between 1960 and 1996, and 15.8 percent between 1962 and 1998.

West Virginia, which experienced an incredible decline in the turnout of its citizens from 78 percent in 1960 to 45 percent in 1996, provides a prototypical example. What made West Virginia's turnout so high in the New Deal and postwar years was likely its party organizations. Certainly it wasn't due to the state's socioeconomic status; the poverty that John F. Kennedy encountered in West Virginia in 1960 was unlike anything he had ever imagined existed in the United States. The secret to Kennedy's famous primary victory in the state was his ability to pay county by county to appear on the list of "slated" candidates.[28] This process was much like contracting—the candidate provided the money and the machine provided the votes it had contracted for. So the poor people of West Virginia came out in heavy numbers because a friend, neighbor, or local official affiliated with their party had asked them to. Indeed, even without any challenge to Nixon in the Republican primary, the turnout of citizens in May 1960 was still above 50 percent. Today's West Virginians are much better off, but without the stimulus of this party organization to get them to the polls, their general election turnout is now consistently below their primary turnout of 1960.

Sweeps of neighborhoods by members of party organizations to get the vote out have been largely replaced by more sophisticated voter targeting. First, campaign literature began to be aimed at specific types of individuals rather than particular precincts. Then it became possible to identify people who were regular voters on the basis of computerized public records. Alan Ware wrote in the mid-1980s that this switch from party to hi-tech campaigning had "helped to create 'two nations' in the electorate: those who received considerable attention from candidates and those who were ignored."[29] With candidates now able to download voter lists off the Internet from Aristotle, Inc., this description of the state of affairs is no doubt even more telling early in the twenty-first century. Ware also went on to speculate that this change in campaigning probably had played some part in the decline of American turnout, a theory that is confirmed by the sharp dropoffs in participation found in the states that formerly had strong party organizations.

In the states that have seen much turnout decline but didn't have strong party organizations, another factor stands out— changes in party competition. Idaho, Utah, and North Dakota have probably seen high levels of turnout decline simply because their elections for major offices have gone from being reasonably competitive to a foregone conclusion. For example, in the early 1960s each of these states had at least one close Senate race, whereas none of them have had a close senatorial contest in recent elections. These states gave Nixon a victory margin ranging from 8 to 11 percent in 1960, but in the equally close national contest of 2000 George W. Bush enjoyed victory margins in them ranging from 28 to 40 percent. As discussed earlier in this chapter, it would be hard for a change in competitiveness of this magnitude not to have some impact on turnout over time.

A multivariate analysis of state turnout change is needed to sort out the independent impact of all the variables that have been reviewed. Table 2.5 displays multiple regression equations predicting changing rates of citizen turnout in the lower forty-eight states for three different time periods, each ranging over at least thirty-six years. (Because of the newness of voting in federal elections in Alaska and Hawaii in the early 1960s, they have been excluded from this analysis; their patterns are anomalies attributable to their special historical situation.) The results of the three equations are strikingly consistent, especially given that two involve presidential contests whereas the other concerns a midterm election. Considering the blunt nature of the traditional party or-

Table 2.5   Multiple regression equations predicting decline in turnout in the lower forty-eight states

	1960 to 1996	1962 to 1998	1960 to 2000
State of party organizations in the 1960s (1 = weak; 5 = strong)	−2.41** (.84)	−1.92* (.85)	−2.38** (.88)
South/non-South (South = 1)	15.28*** (3.06)	14.83*** (2.97)	18.37*** (2.96)
Change in contested and close races index	1.93* (.93)	4.12*** (1.10)	1.66 (.87)
Number of days before election day to register in 1996–2000 period	.06 (.14)	−.17 (.14)	.00 (.14)
Constant	−9.96** (3.02)	−4.27 (3.09)	−7.56* (3.14)
N	48	48	48
Multiple R	.78	.78	.77
R²	.61	.61	.59

***$p < .001$.   **$p < .01$.   *$p < .05$.

ganization score and the competitiveness index, the fact that 60 percent of the variance can be explained is impressive.

The variable with the largest impact is naturally the South/non-South one, as would be expected given the fact that many southern states have bucked the national tide of declining turnout. It would be hard to dispute the argument that changes in voter registration procedures in the South explain much of this phenomenon. Yet it should be kept in mind that these were openly discriminatory provisions of voter registration procedures, designed to keep people out the system. The closing-date provisions that are currently the subject of scholarly attention are of marginal consequence by comparison, merely making it somewhat more convenient for the minority of citizens who are not already registered to do so in time to vote. The insignificant coefficient for the closing-date variable in each of the three equations in Table 2.5 contradicts the theory that turnout decline would be ameliorated over time by lenient registration deadlines. Rather than registration laws making a difference in turnout of approximately 9 percent, as argued by Wolfinger and Rosenstone, the decline of party organizations since the 1960s has had this level of impact in the reverse direction. With each increase in Mayhew's five-step coding regarding traditional party organizations, turnout declined by an additional 2.4 percent in presidential election years.[30] Controlling for all the other factors, one would thus expect a state that had a very strong party organization in the 1960s to experience presidential-year turnout decline of 9.6 percent more than a state that had little semblance of such organizations. The impact of party organizations is somewhat less in the midterm comparison between 1962 and 1998, but in this equation the index of close and contested races is of greater consequence. Given the lower degree of media attention to campaigns in midterm elections, it makes sense that having major, close contests on the ballot would be more important in predicting turnout change. In both presidential and midterm years, there is a notable decline in the mean value of this competitiveness variable over time, which has thus contributed in part to the decline of turnout nationwide.[31]

Conclusion

In a statistical sense, the profound turnout decline in the states that had strong party organizations may simply represent regression to the mean, as campaigning throughout the nation has become more homogenized. But this point does not diminish the political significance of the waning ability of traditional party organizations to mobilize people to vote. Without the mobilization efforts of political machines and the team spirit they engendered, turnout has gone down dramatically in these areas of the country. Of course, all of the nonsouthern states in the continental United States have seen at least some degree of turnout decline since the early 1960s. More than party organizational decline is at the root of declining turnout in these states. National trends, such as the decline of social capital, are no doubt at work.

It is often said that states are laboratories for policy innovation within the United States. Although many states have experimented with policies designed to improve voter turnout, no clear success story can yet be identified. Oregon has recently tried all-mail balloting, but this has only had a noteworthy impact in increasing turnout for low-salience elections.[32] Many states have experimented with early voting, but voting early has not led to voting often.[33] Absentee voting has been made easier in many states, such as California's provision that no reason is necessary in order to receive a mail ballot, but again the results have been disappointing. After reviewing state experiences with early and mail voting, the National Commission on Federal Election Reform remarked that it was troubled by this trend. Commission members noted that voting by mail is typically adopted as a means for improving turnout, "but often seems to be motivated at least as much by considerations of administrative convenience and saving money."[34] The commission rightly pointed out that the price of this administrative efficiency is the diminution of the community ritual of voting—a development that has probably not helped the turnout rates of people with marginal interest in politics.

Most important, federal efforts to make it easier to register to vote have added more people to the voter rolls but without the desired result of getting more people to actually vote. The answer to the paradox of easier registration and lower turnout appears to be that registration is simply not that important a factor, provided that the laws are not openly discriminatory—as they were during the Jim Crow period in the South. Most people who want to vote will manage to register. Getting people on the registration rolls with relatively little interest in politics has apparently accomplished little, as they are not very likely to vote. Nor has making it possible to register on election day had much impact on turnout rates (except in extraordinary circumstances—such as engendered by Jesse Ventura's engaging campaign for governor of Minnesota in 1998).

After the low turnout in the first election in which the national Motor Voter law was in place, some members of Congress called for its repeal. But repeal would be a mistake, even though the law has not had its desired impact thus far. To repeal the law could well be interpreted as indicating that the country is giving up on ways to increase turnout, and therefore is content with participation rates of about 50 percent. Besides, one never knows when a sudden event, such as the controversy over the counting of ballots in 2000, might suddenly motivate nonvoters who are on the registration rolls to start participating. Similarly, even though the loosening of registration closing dates has not stemmed the tide of falling turnout rates over time, it would be sensible to continue this policy trend wherever it is feasible to do so without inviting fraud. With sophisticated computer technology making it possible to update registration files more expeditiously, people should be given the maximum feasible amount of time to register. Getting a higher percentage of individuals who are registered to actually vote, however, remains a problem that is not likely to be solved at the state level. Examining what sorts of individuals have been dropping out of the electorate thus becomes warranted.

CHAPTER THREE

Types of Individuals Who Vote

One general pattern identifies the types of individual Americans who have voted at the highest rates in recent elections: those for whom voting is user friendly. Furthermore, this pattern is more clearly evident now than it was in the era of higher turnout in the 1960s. The decline in turnout is therefore traceable at the individual level to the sorts of individuals who do not find the act of voting particularly rewarding.

Although this may seem to be a tautological assertion that the kinds of people who don't vote are those who don't want to, there is far more to it than that. Because this is a trend in American electoral behavior rather than a constant, people who for one reason or another can readily see benefits to voting are being better represented at the polls, whereas those who cannot so easily perceive such benefits are losing clout. Such a development is quite compatible with the previous chapter's finding that the decline of party machines accounts for a good portion of turnout decline in the states; machines formerly facilitated the turnout of people with marginal political interest and/or commitments. The findings of this chapter are also nicely compatible with the null findings regarding the importance of state registration laws. By making registration easier, it was thought that people with lesser education, life experience, political interest, and partisanship would become more likely to vote. As this chapter will show, these are precisely the types of individuals whose turnout rates have fallen the most. Such unanticipated trends lend further credence to the argument that making the registration process easier is not the solution to America's turnout woes. Rather, it is the act of voting itself that has become less user friendly to a variety of types of individuals, and therefore needs attention.

Understanding why some people vote and others do not is a difficult task. Just as a physicist cannot predict with certainty how any specific molecule will react in an experiment, so political scientists cannot say for certain who will vote and who will not. But just as physicists can assess probabilities of how molecules will move, so political scientists can assess the chances that an individual with certain characteristics and attitudes will vote. Explaining why some people vote and others do not has attracted a variety of social scientific approaches. Chief among them are economic, psychological, and sociological theories. I will examine a variety of factors under each of these rubrics with regard to explaining who presently votes in the United States as compared with the early 1960s.

The Economic/Rational Choice Approach to Turnout

The fundamental axiom of economic theory as it applies to voting is that citizens act rationally as they make their decisions about whether or not to vote.[1] Just as they do for any consumer purchase, people are hypothesized to consider both the costs and the benefits. If the benefits outweigh the costs, then the rational choice is to vote. Thus if turnout is declining, it must be because the benefits no longer outweigh the costs for many people.

Although this theory is simple and straightforward, in practice every voter probably weighs the various costs and benefits somewhat differently. A benefit that one person sees as worth trudging through a blizzard for in order to vote may not be considered of much value by another person. Similarly, a cost that might seem incredibly burdensome to one individual might be only a minor annoyance to another. Nevertheless, it is useful to outline the major costs and benefits that citizens must consider in deciding whether to vote. For example, if the costs and benefits that Americans encounter are markedly different than those encountered by citizens of other countries, then that should help explain why the U.S. turnout rate is so low. How these factors have differentially affected various groups will be addressed in subsequent sections on psychological and sociological theories.

The Costs of Voting

In the literature on U.S. voting, more attention has been given to the costs than to the benefits, probably because one cost has drawn overwhelming attention—that of registration. Wolfinger and Rosenstone argued that "the more permissive the registration laws, the lower the time, energy, and information costs of voting."[2] The data presented in the previous chapter have shown that registration is a relatively minor factor in calculating the overall cost of voting for most citizens. It is likely, however, that the general factors that Wolfinger and Rosenstone cite—time, energy, and information costs—are substantial in and of themselves.

In particular, the information costs that Americans typically encounter as they decide whether or not to vote are often overwhelming. As I look at what I am asked to vote on in California in gubernatorial years, I find that even as a political science professor, my level of political information is inadequate to deal with the many questions at stake. For example, I've voted for state controller in four elections, but I've yet to learn what the holder of this office actually does. When I ask my students, the answer I always get back is "He (or she) controls." Usually, I can prod someone into saying that the controller deals with money. But students are stumped when I ask how this position differs from state treasurer, which is also an elected office. I then pose further rhetorical questions, such as what are the issues in the campaigns for state insurance commissioner, superintendent of schools, or secretary of state, and whether class members know anything about the judges we have to decide whether to retain. Finally, I read a few complicated California propositions to them, such as two votes in 2000 on insurance claims practices. By the time I finish, I think I've made my point: all of these demands on citizens probably discourage many people from voting in the first place. As mentioned in Chapter 1, cross-national data support this theory, because Switzerland—the only other established democracy to place so many demands on its citizens at the polls—also has very low turnout rates.

An additional important cost that must be considered is the time it takes to get to the polls and go through the physical process of voting. As shown in Table 3.1, the most frequent response given by registered nonvoters in the 1996 Census Bureau survey was that they were too busy—a reason that was given almost three times as frequently as in 1980. The fact that elections are traditionally held in the United States on Tuesday is another reason why the American voting process is not user friendly. It is true that those who know they are going to be busy all day can vote ahead of time in many states. Yet many people cannot predict how much free time they will have on a given Tuesday. On the Monday before an election one might think one would have sufficient time the following day, but an unexpected cell phone call, email, incoming fax, or the vibration of a beeper can easily change that situation. It is probably no coincidence that as the

Table 3.1   Reasons for not voting among those registered (in percent)

	1980	1996
Too busy; could not take time off from work/school	7.6	21.5
Not interested	11.2	16.6
Sick/disabled/family emergency	17.1	14.9
Did not prefer any of the candidates	16.0	13.0
Out of town	12.6	11.1
Other reasons	17.2	15.9
Had no way to get to the polls	4.1	4.3
Don't know; refused to answer	14.1	2.7

Source: U.S. Census Bureau surveys.

pace of modern life has accelerated, more people are finding that they are too busy to vote, or at least figure that is their best excuse.

The Benefits of Voting
In civics classes, most Americans are taught that they should vote because every vote can make a difference. Realistically, when over 100 million people vote in a presidential election, as they did in 2000, the chance that one vote will affect the outcome is extraordinarily slight. Once in a while, of course, an election is decided by a handful of votes, as occurred in Florida in 2000—where the 0.009 percent margin between Bush and Gore was less than the margin of error created by less than completely reliable methods of recording votes. It is more likely, however, that an individual will be struck by lightning at some point in his or her lifetime than participate in an election decided by a single vote.

This fact raises one of the great paradoxes in the literature on turnout: why should anyone bother to vote, given the sheer improbability of a single vote's making a difference? William Riker and Peter Ordeshook's classic answer to this question was that some people vote out of a sense of civic duty, knowing full well that they have no chance to influence the outcome.[3] Rather than enjoying the short-term gain of electing one's favorite candidates, the benefit from doing one's civic duty is the long-term contribution made toward preserving democracy. As Donald Green and Ian Shapiro argue, however, there is no explanation for why the practice of civic duty should result in widely different turnout rates for national as opposed to local elections.[4]

Another problem with the notion of civic duty is that virtually all Americans express these values, regardless of whether they themselves vote. When presented with the statement that "so many other people vote in national elections that it doesn't matter much to me whether I vote or not," 92 percent disagreed in 1960 and 91 percent did so in 1980. In 1960, 93 percent rejected the statement that "it isn't so important to vote when you know your party can't win," and in 1980 the figure was barely changed at 92 percent. With these results, it is hard to imagine that feelings of civic duty explain why so few Americans vote or why turnout has been going down.[5]

Nevertheless, as Bernard Grofman has pointed out, rational choice theory can be of some use in explaining marginal changes in turnout rates over time.[6] An important class of benefits that voters receive is the value of expressing their support for various positions, candidates, and groups. In other words, many people vote simply because for one reason or another they care who wins. Such participation can be likened to spectators at sporting event. Just as with voting, the involvement of any particular fan is hardly crucial to the outcome. But at the same time, just as a game without fans would lack a homefield advantage, so democracy wouldn't exist without at least some citizens going to the polls. Individually, sports spectators get the selective benefits of being able to root in person for their team, enjoy the spectacle, and see who wins. Similar benefits can be posited for voters. People who have a clear personal interest in who governs and what government policies are adopted should be more likely to feel that there is a benefit to voting, in the same way that people with a favorite team are more apt to attend a sporting event. As shown in Table 3.1, two of the major reasons respondents chose for not voting in 1996 were a lack of interest and the fact that they didn't prefer any of the candidates.

An overall reduction in the benefits of political expression provides the most plausible source for turnout decline from an economic perspective. After all, the benefits of influencing the election and doing one's civic duty have not changed, and the costs of registering and voting have either decreased or stayed about the same. Because expressive benefits are primarily psychological, examining the relationship between turnout and various attitudes that provide incentives to vote is a logical next step.

Psychological Predictors of Voting Turnout

Angus Campbell and his colleagues wrote decades ago in *The American Voter* that "the decision to vote, no less than the decision to vote for a given party, rests immediately on psychological forces."[7] The major forces they identified were strength of party identification, political interest, caring about the outcome, and political efficacy—all of which continue to be relevant today. Indeed, in line with the argument that expressive benefits are most important in understanding why turnout has declined, three of these four psychological variables are more related to turnout in the 1990s than in the 1960s. The exception is political efficacy (that is, the perception that one can make a difference in politics), which is an attitude that taps resources much more than benefits.[8]

Table 3.2 presents National Election Studies data from the 1960 and 1996 presidential elections and the midterm elections of 1962 and 1998 that illustrate how these psychological factors af-

Table 3.2 Standardized turnout figures by psychological variables in the 1960s and 1990s

	1960	1996	1962	1998
Strong party identifiers	+8	+24	+19	+39
Weak party identifiers	+2	−3	−3	−11
Independent leaners	−1	−8	−8	−17
Pure Independents	−28	−42	−40	−32
Very much interested in campaign	+14	+32	+29	+60
Somewhat interested in campaign	+3	+1	+2	−1
Not much interested in campaign	−29	−33	−44	−39
Care who wins	+9	+9	N.A.	+32
Don't care who wins	−18	−33	N.A.	−35
High efficacy	+14	+19	N.A.	+30
Medium efficacy	0	+3	N.A.	+5
Low efficacy	−34	−9	N.A.	−15

Note and Sources: Each entry is calculated by taking the turnout rate of the group and comparing it with the average for all the survey respondents in that year. For example, if a group had a turnout rate of 50 percent and the national average were 55 percent, it would receive a score of −10. Data are from the National Election Studies. *N.A.* = Not available.

fected reported turnout. These numbers are standardized according to the average turnout rate for the entire sample in each year. For example, if 77 percent of a particular group said they voted as compared with an overall rate of 70 percent, then the standardized turnout would be 10 percent above average, as represented by +10 in the table notation. The focus of the analysis is on the relative impact of the independent variables rather than on the raw NES turnout numbers, which consistently overestimate participation and underestimate the magnitude of turnout decline.[9]

At the heart of the psychological approach to turnout is party identification. Warren Miller notes that the concept was designed to be similar to religious affiliation, and the term "identification" was "used quite intentionally to express the assumption that the relationship often involves an extension of ego."[10] As such, people with a stronger party identification are bound to think they have more at stake on election day. If one identifies with a party, then when that party wins one wins along with it. Furthermore, the perceptual screening function of partisanship enables one to easily interpret the complex political world and thus lessens the informational costs associated with voting.

Ironically, the decline of American political parties in recent decades has made strength of partisanship even more important in predicting who votes. Table 3.2 shows that over time, the turnout gap between strong party identifiers and Independents has grown significantly. The rise of candidate-centered politics and the decline of partisanship may well explain this phenomenon.[11] When the focus of campaigns was on the two parties rather than on the many candidates for many offices, everyone gained at least somewhat from lower information costs. In addition, when even many Independents cast a straight ticket, the benefits were much clearer to see than those derived from picking and choosing one's favorite candidates from both parties. Thus even those who didn't identify with a party in 1960 could benefit from the partisan manner with which campaigns were conducted. In today's candidate-centered environment, the mobilizing effects of party competition have been felt more disproportionately according to one's level of party identification. The result has been rising inequality of turnout rates according to partisan strength.

Identifying with a party also makes people more likely to find campaigns interesting and to care who wins. Each of these variables makes its own contribution to the turnout decision. Warren Miller and J. Merrill Shanks bluntly state that "it is not hard to understand why most non-voters don't vote: they are uninterested, uninformed, and uninvolved."[12] Table 3.2 shows that this state of affairs was substantially more evident in the 1990s than in the 1960s. In other words, turnout has declined because people who are indifferent about the outcome and uninterested in the campaign are no longer being as effectively mobilized. These sorts of people have always been on the periphery of American politics, but now are more so. Parties once mobilized many of these people through grassroots activity, but in most localities, no longer do.

The failure to mobilize peripheral voters appears to be more a problem of motivation than of resources, as evidenced by the fact that political efficacy was less related to turnout in 1996 than in 1960. When registration barriers were difficult to overcome, feeling that one had the ability to make a difference in politics was more vital in determining turnout. With registration now being much more user friendly, a low sense of political efficacy is naturally less of an impediment to voting. The fact that efficacy has declined in recent decades has certainly played some role in the decline of turnout, but in today's political world it may not be as important as it was in the past.[13]

Thus far, the economic approach has shown that decreasing benefits rather than rising costs are at the root of America's turnout problem. The psychological approach has further identified the problem to be primarily one of a lack of motivation to vote, particularly stemming from party decline. These conclusions are further confirmed by an examination of sociological factors related to turnout.

Sociological Predictors of Voting Turnout

Immediately following an election, politicians want to know what sort of people did or did not vote. In particular, newly elected officeholders need to assess the makeup of the coalition that put them into office in order to start working on keeping these people satisfied and ready to reelect them. Losing politicians, by contrast, want to know if their biggest supporters did not make it to the polls, and hence whether their failure was more a problem of mobilization than of message.

The best source of data on the demographics of who votes can be found in the biennial surveys conducted by the Census Bureau as part of the Current Population Survey since 1964. These surveys have the great advantages of: (1) a huge sample size of at least 50,000 individuals; and (2) a very high response rate of approximately 95 percent.[14] However, because only age, education, race, and gender are available from Census data going back to 1964, NES data will be added here for other relevant demographic variables. The data presented in Table 3.3 allow comparisons of the relative impact of variables from different data sources (given that they are all standardized according to the overall turnout rate in each particular survey).

Universal suffrage means that everyone should have an equal opportunity to vote, regardless of social background. But since the 1960s, Table 3.3 shows that in many respects social biases in voting participation have increased. One exception to this pattern involves the data for men versus women. For decades after the nationwide enfranchisement of women in 1920, political scientists noted women's lower participation rates in elections. By the mid-1960s, female turnout rates had at long last nearly caught up to those of males. According to the Census surveys, in the late 1990s women actually had slightly higher turnout rates than men, though the differences are so slight that without the precision allowed by the large Census samples it would scarcely be worth mentioning.

The primary purpose of instituting Census Bureau studies of registration and turnout was to monitor racial patterns in electoral participation, because there was much concern about the lack of Black political participation. Since these studies were be-

Table 3.3 Standardized turnout figures for demographic groups in the 1960s and 1990s

	1964	1996	1966	1998
No high school	−15	−45	−19	−43
Some high school	−6	−38	−10	−41
High school graduate	+10	−11	+8	−11
Some college	+18	+12	+17	+10
College graduate	+26	+34	+27	+36
Age				
18–20	N.A.	−42	N.A.	−68
21–24	−26	−38	−43	−46
25–44	0	−9	−4	−17
45–64	+10	+19	+16	+28
65+	−4	+24	+1	+42
White	+2	+3	+3	+3
Black	−16	−7	−25	−5
Hispanic citizens	N.A.	−19	N.A.	−23
Asian citizens	N.A.	−17	N.A.	−23
Male	+2	−3	+5	−1
Female	−3	+2	−4	+1
Married	+1	+12	+7	+14
Unmarried	−5	−18	−18	−20
Less than four years in residence	−9	−11	−19	−32
More than four years in residence	+8	+9	+17	+23
Union household	+7	+15	+1	+26
Nonunion household	−2	−3	−1	−5
Attend religious services regularly	+7	+16	+18	+26
Attend religious services often	+3	−3	−3	−6
Seldom attend religious services	−7	−2	−14	−3
Never attend religious services	−18	−18	−12	−27

Note and Sources: Each entry is calculated by taking the turnout rate of the group and comparing it with the average for all the survey respondents in that year. For example, if a group had a turnout rate of 50 percent and the national average were 55 percent, it would receive a score of −10. Data on age, education, race, and gender are from the Census Bureau studies; data on marital status, residential mobility, union membership, and religious attendance are from the National Election Studies. *N.A.* = Not available.

gun, the gap between White and Black turnout rates has narrowed considerably, as legal barriers to Black participation have
come down. In their classic study of political participation, Sidney Verba and Norman Nie argued that, controlling for socioeconomic status, Blacks actually participated at higher rates than
Whites as a result of racial group consciousness.[15] This finding led
many teachers to speculate that eventually Black participation
might exceed that of Whites as Blacks made progress in narrow-
ing the educational gap. In recent Census studies, however,
Blacks report higher turnout levels than Whites only at educational levels below that of high school graduate.

Nevertheless, it is possible to see evidence of group mobilization among Blacks in recent years through an examination of actual records of registration and voting. Because of the requirements of the Voting Rights Act, some states are required to ask for
racial information on their voter registration forms. I was able to
find two localities, a state and a large county, that report the actual registration and turnout counts by race and party registration. In these two areas it is thus possible to precisely assess the
turnout rate of a rare political breed—Black Republicans. One
might expect Black Republicans to be highly participatory because they have gone against the grain of their ethnic group in
declaring their party registration, which might be interpreted as
showing a fair degree of contemplation about politics. As can be
seen by the number of Black voters in each category in Table 3.4,
Democrats outnumber Republicans by about twenty to one in
both Louisiana and Miami-Dade County. Furthermore, data are
available on turnout rates by party registration in many localities,
and GOP partisans are usually slightly more likely to vote. However, this is certainly not the case among Black Republicans. In
both Louisiana and Miami, their turnout rates are at least 15 percentage points lower than those of Black Democrats. In fact,
Black Republicans are scarcely more likely to vote than are Black

Table 3.4 Turnout percentages by party registration/race in Miami and Louisiana. (Numbers in parentheses are actual number of voters registered in that category.)

	Republicans	Democrats	Nonpartisans
Miami-Dade 1998			
Whites	45.2	53.8	32.5
	(99,850)	(145,041)	(45,971)
Blacks	33.2	48.5	27.3
	(7,508)	(148,192)	(14,862)
Hispanics	56.9	40.2	34.4
	(206,550)	(85,480)	(59,729)
Other race	40.9	33.8	24.9
	(6,989)	(10,229)	(7,276)
Louisiana 2000			
Whites	71.1	69.6	50.8
	(570,063)	(977,066)	(347,828)
Blacks	41.3	62.4	38.3
	(28,622)	(670,337)	(110,244)
Other race	57.4	51.4	37.4
	(18,297)	(27,240)	(46,854)

Sources: Official numbers provided by Miami-Dade County supervisor of elections and the Louisiana Department of Elections and Registration.

nonpartisans. It is almost as if they had no party affiliation at all. Because their racial identification is at odds with their party identification, race is probably not very politicized for these citizens. Furthermore, they are not likely to be mobilized by turnout efforts in their community.

A similar pattern can be found for Hispanics in Miami, the majority of whom are Cubans whose virulent anticommunism has propelled them into strong support for the GOP. These Hispanic Republicans in fact recorded the highest turnout rate for any racial/party combination shown in Table 3.4 for Miami. In contrast, Hispanics who were in the minority in registering as

Democrats scarcely had higher turnout rates than Hispanic non-partisans. Further evidence supporting the notion that the mobilization of racial minorities partly depends on racial identifications matching the dominant partisanship of one's group can be seen by turning to an area where Democratic identification is the norm among Hispanics. In Orange County, California, where those with Hispanic surnames or who were born in Latin America register as Democrats over Republicans at a rate greater than two to one, it is the Democrats who have higher turnout rates.[16]

Overall, the Census data for Hispanics indicate that their growing numbers in the U.S. population in recent decades have contributed somewhat to the decline of turnout. Hispanic citizens in 1996 and 1998 reported turnout rates approximately 20 percent lower than the national average. And of course the influx of Hispanic noncitizens has inevitably lowered turnout rates, as current state laws do not allow resident aliens to vote. Nevertheless, the case of Hispanic Republicans in Miami certainly points toward optimism about Latino participation if they can be more fully incorporated into their political communities. Given demographic projections that Hispanics will make up a quarter of the population by the year 2050, there is every reason to expect that the political parties should make efforts in this direction.

Asian Americans are also expected to increase rapidly as a percentage of the population, and at present their turnout patterns are fairly similar to those of Hispanics. Many are noncitizens, and even among those who have attained citizenship, the turnout rate is about 20 percent below the national average according to the Census surveys. Most of the people who classify themselves as being of an "other" race in Miami are probably Asian (in Louisiana, this category is probably a mixture of Hispanics and Asians), and their turnout rate is low. For example, in Orange County, California, those who report being born in Asia on their registration forms have turnout rates about 10 percent below the county average for those on the registration rolls. But as with Hispanics, there is reason to be optimistic about Asian-American participation levels in the future. Among the racial groups that collectively are projected to make up the so-called minority-majority in the mid-twenty-first century, Asian Americans are often called the "superachievers." This is especially true in the case of educational attainment—42 percent of Asian Americans over the age of twenty-five currently have a college degree, almost twice the national average. With such high levels of education, it is to be expected that their turnout rates will eventually rise substantially as they become better integrated into American political communities.

Integration into one's community is a central factor in making everyone—not just racial minorities—aware of the benefits of voting. A number of variables in Table 3.3 bolster this point. Two important factors that promote a sense of belonging to one's local neighborhood are being married and maintaining a stable residence. In the case of residential mobility, Peverill Squire and his colleagues argued that movers have low turnout rates because of the need to re-register.[17] The Motor Voter bill has done away with much of the hassle of re-registering, yet even after controlling for age, mobility remains a significant factor in predicting turnout. Such a finding indicates that movers' low turnout is mostly due to a lack of what Ruy Teixeira terms "social connectedness"—ties that "provide external encouragement to vote, as well an enhanced sense of an election's meaningfulness."[18]

One might theorize that being married doubles social connectedness. Mark Gray has shown through a careful analysis of actual voter history records that people who live in a household with someone else who votes are much more likely to vote themselves, even controlling for a host of political and demographic factors. As Gray aptly puts it, people frequently vote in pairs.[19] Although not the only means of pairing up, marriage is certainly the most common, and the best way of assessing this phenomenon over time. By the late 1990s, a large gap had opened up be-

tween those who were married and those who were not with respect to turnout. The substantial decline in marriage rates is one
of the chief demographic causes of turnout decline.

Within one's community, there are numerous groups one can
belong to that can contribute to social connectedness. Naturally,
belonging to social groups that are involved in politics increases
one's likelihood of voting. Both unions and churches have long
been active in the political process and often devote group resources to turning their members out to vote. Although both
have experienced membership declines in recent decades, the
data indicate that such group incentives have actually become
more effective in today's low turnout environment.

The two best demographic predictors of turnout—age and education—also contribute toward social connectedness, but their
roles in promoting electoral participation extend well beyond
this facet. Young people have always had the lowest turnout
rates, which is perhaps the reason why there was relatively little
opposition to lowering the voting age to eighteen in the early
1970s. But even the most pessimistic analysts could not have
foreseen the record low participation rates of Generation X. As
shown in Table 3.3, the turnout rate for people under twenty-five
was about 40 percent below the national average in 1996, and
was even worse in 1998. In contrast, senior citizens have moved
from average turnout rates in the 1960s to very high levels in recent years. Thus America has seen a huge age gap develop in voting participation. This gap is of such magnitude and importance
that the following chapter will be devoted exclusively to this
topic.

The Education-Turnout Puzzle

The extraordinarily low turnout rates of today's young citizens
seems paradoxical, given that they are one of the best-educated

generations in American history. As Wolfinger and Rosenstone demonstrated in their classic study, people with higher levels of education are more likely to: (1) express a high sense of citizen duty; (2) say they are very interested in politics; (3) follow the news closely; and (4) be well informed about politics.[20] All of these factors increase the benefits of voting and therefore make participation more likely. In particular, it is self-evident that people who know enough to realize where their true political interests lie should be the most likely to vote.

Why, then, should turnout be going down at the same time that educational levels are going up nationwide? Had turnout rates within each educational level stayed the same as they were in 1964, the rise of educational achievement in the population would have boosted national turnout rates by 10 percentage points by 2000. The fact that turnout has gone down as the electorate has become more educated is probably the most puzzling facet of the phenomenon of turnout decline in the United States since the early 1960s.

Norman Nie, Jane Junn, and Kenneth Stehlik-Barry propose a seemingly ingenious solution to this puzzle: it is not the absolute level of education that matters with regard to political participation, but rather someone's educational ranking within his or her own generation. They suggest that "formal education is important to the characteristics of political engagement because it sorts individual citizens into positions in the social and political hierarchy that facilitate political engagement to a greater or lesser degree."[21] In other words, it's not how much you know, but more precisely how much you know compared with everyone else. According to this theory, the impact of having a college degree on political participation should have been reduced in recent decades, because this has become a far more common educational achievement. Many parents and grandparents have discovered to their dismay that a college education doesn't guarantee success the way it used to. An increase in educational achievement nationwide should therefore have no impact on participation according to Nie and his colleagues, because only a fixed proportion can be near the top of the political heap at a given time.

A critical feature of the sorting model employed by Nie, Junn, and Stehlik-Barry, is their assertion that "certain aspects of democratic citizenship are in fact bounded, or limited, by their essential competitive nature."[22] If half the American voting-age population were to contribute $100 to a presidential candidate, for example, that would provide $100 billion to run the campaign—far more than the candidates could reasonably use by any stretch of the imagination. Similarly, if half the people who voted for each member of Congress were to write that representative an email or letter every year, that would produce more mail than could be read with anything near current staffing levels, much less answered. Or if half the population were to try to personally attend a political meeting during each congressional campaign, candidates would have to regularly rent out sports arenas to deal with the crowds, and few voters would actually get any personal contact with the candidate.

Although the sorting model might make some sense in predicting political activity that requires a fair degree of personal initiative, such as those mentioned above, it makes little sense with regard to turnout. It is safe to say that no established democracy has seen anything like half of the population giving money to campaigns or attending meetings, but as shown in Chapter 1, a number of countries have recently experienced turnout rates above 80 percent. Any premise that voting participation is somehow bounded (other than at 100 percent) is clearly inappropriate. In fact, in most other established democracies education is hardly related to turnout at all. Figure 3.1 shows the degree of this relationship in all the advanced industrialized democracies included thus far in the Comparative Study of Electoral Systems (CSES)

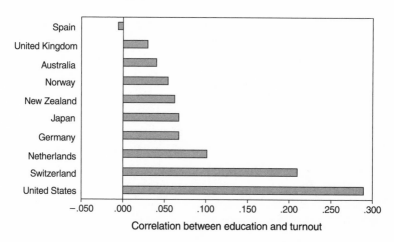

Figure 3.1 Correlation between education and turnout in advanced industrialized democracies in recent years. (Data from Comparative Study of Electoral Systems.)

project. Whereas in the United States education levels explain over 8 percent of the variance in turnout, in all the other countries besides Switzerland it explains no more than 1 percent.

Why do the United States and Switzerland stand out among established democracies in having substantially higher turnout levels among those with more education? The answer is that both have the distinction of not being very user-friendly political systems. Writing about turnout around the world, the Canadian political scientist André Blais states that "few would argue that voting is a very demanding activity."[23] Such an assertion is certainly true in most countries where a voter is confronted with the task of making only one or two marks on a ballot, but nowhere in the United States is voting in major elections anywhere near that simple. Education helps U.S. voters navigate long and often complex ballots in a way that is not relevant in other OECD-member democracies aside from Switzerland.

Several decades ago, many Americans with lower levels of education were often mobilized to vote on behalf of their political party. With the weakening of partisanship since then, these same individuals have been set adrift in the ebb and flow of today's political world without an anchor that would help them realize the benefits of voting. If this is indeed the case, then education should have become even more related to turnout in recent years in the United States. In contrast, the sorting hypothesis would predict that turnout should be less related to education over time as we have become a more educationally homogeneous society.[24] As a college education has become more common, the sorting hypothesis would lead one to expect that such an achievement would provide less of a boost to turnout than it used to. But as can be seen in Table 3.3, just the opposite has been the case. College graduates have become even more likely to vote compared with the national average, and those without a high school degree have dropped off the charts in terms of voting participation. As a result, in 1996 people without any college education made up 52 percent of the adult population but only 41 percent of the voters. By comparison, in 1964 their underrepresentation was much less. Those who had not gone to college in 1964 constituted 80 percent of all adults and 76 percent of those who went to the polls.

If the sorting hypothesis of Nie and his colleagues were correct, then we would expect to find that turnout will be less related to education among younger than among older citizens, as the standard deviation for educational achievement has shrunk with each succeeding age group in recent decades. But again, just the opposite is the case. What Nie and his colleagues fail to take notice of is the interaction between age and education in American turnout patterns. As Wolfinger and Rosenstone noted in their detailed analysis of the 1972 Census survey, "the effect of age on the probability of voting is greatest among those with the least

Table 3.5 Correlation between age and turnout controlling for education levels

	Less than 8 years	8–11 years	High school diploma	Some college	B.A.	Advanced degree
1972	.158	.272	.213	.138	.072	.086
1996	.343	.347	.302	.246	.170	.150
1974	.182	.265	.298	.261	.193	.188
1998	.309	.359	.335	.327	.260	.237

Source: U.S. Census Bureau studies.

schooling."[25] This interaction is even clearer in the Census data from the late 1990s, as shown in Table 3.5. The more educated one is, the less position in the life cycle matters in predicting turnout. Basically, higher education provides the knowledge necessary to realize the benefits of voting that otherwise takes the accumulation of lifetime experiences to acquire, as people learn how the political system affects them and who best represents their interests. For example, in 1996 someone with a college degree who was twenty-five to thirty-one years of age was already just as likely to vote as a fifty-three- to fifty-nine-year-old with just a high school diploma. With such a steep learning curve, the relationship between age and turnout is necessarily limited at higher levels of education.

Therefore, the decline in turnout should be found to be concentrated among younger citizens with the lowest levels of education. Table 3.6 displays percentage-point declines in turnout by age/education categories from the first archived Census surveys in 1972 to that of 1996.[26] The patterns are clear-cut. With the exception of senior citizens, whose turnout rates have scarcely diminished at all, in each age category the decline is more pronounced among the less educated. And within each educational

Table 3.6 Percentage point changes in turnout by age and education, 1972–1996

	Less than 8 years	8–11 years	High school diploma	Some college	B.A.	Advanced degree
25–31	−13	−17	−27	−25	−20	−20
32–38	−18	−23	−27	−17	−17	−13
39–45	−25	−26	−24	−16	−13	−9
46–52	−21	−25	−23	−14	−11	−8
53–59	−18	−22	−14	−9	−8	−9
60–66	−12	−19	−7	−6	−1	−2
67–73	−1	−6	−4	−2	−4	−5
74–80	+5	−5	+3	0	−3	−8

Source: U.S. Census Bureau studies.

category, the decline in turnout is more pronounced at younger ages. Thus a big part of the answer to the question of who is voting less is *young people with lower levels of education*. Understanding the role that age has played is crucial to any examination of turnout decline, and will be examined in considerable depth in the following chapter.

Conclusion

The story of the rich becoming richer and the poor becoming poorer has become an increasingly common one in American society in recent decades. Although we are a long way away from what Robert Frank and Philip Cook call the "winner-take-all society"[27] in terms of voting, there has been movement in that direction. The major message of this chapter is that those who are resource rich have become richer in terms of representation at the polls. Those who are not very interested in politics, not very partisan, not very well educated, and not very old have dropped out of the active electorate at alarming rates. These groups are among the least likely to see the benefits of voting, and consequently are being increasingly underrepresented in the electoral process. But democracy is not just for the politically interested, the partisans, the well educated, the elderly, and so on. A democratic system is supposed to enable all to have their voices heard and their interests represented. And whether people realize it or not, everyone has something at stake in the political process and some interests to be represented. Nie, Junn, and Stehlik-Barry argue that because the relative costs and benefits of being politically active vary according to educational ranking, equality of political access can never be fully achieved.[28] This state of affairs may well be true with respect to political activities that require a good deal of effort and/or skill. But it should not be the case for voting. Other countries have created electoral structures where there are only minor inequalities in voting participation, as shown by the cross-national data reviewed here regarding turnout patterns by education.

A consistent finding with regard to inequalities in American turnout patterns is that they are more pronounced in midterm than in presidential elections. Most likely this stems from the principle that the fewer people that vote the worse representation is likely to be. If this is the case, then it is likely that turnout in very low turnout elections such as primaries and special elections will see even more extreme biases in terms of who votes. The following chapter will demonstrate that this is indeed the case for age and turnout, for which very precise data are available through public records.

The New Generation Gap

In November of 1998 I did not vote. Like many of my fellow baby boomers, I was relatively nonchalant about failing to participate. In my own mind, I felt that I had a pretty good excuse. About a week before the election my father had undergone heart bypass surgery. I had flown across the country on short notice to be there, and the thought of getting an absentee ballot before I left California was not something that crossed my mind. (By the time I arrived on the East Coast it was too late to request an absentee ballot by mail, but I later realized I could have requested one in person just before I left.) Ironically, I was able to keep a few commitments on election day to do radio interviews on the topic of nonvoting by simply emailing the producers that I would be at a different phone number. The fact that I wasn't voting that day came up a couple times on the air and led to further interesting discussion, but no real embarrassment on my part.

My father, by contrast, took a different view regarding not voting. He had just gotten out of the hospital a couple of days before the election and had scarcely been able to walk ten yards outside the house, but nevertheless said on Tuesday morning that he wanted to be driven to the polls. This idea did not sound wise to me under the circumstances. I proposed an alternative—given that my parents were going to vote for different candidates for governor, I suggested that neither one vote rather than going to the trouble of canceling each other out. This suggestion met with resistance from both my parents, who reminded me that there were many offices on the ballot besides governor and that they probably would agree on some of them. Yet they acknowledged that without the use of a wheelchair it would be very difficult for my father to make it from the curb to the high school gym where their community votes. We agreed that I would first go to the polling place and see if there was a wheelchair there. When I returned from my scouting trip I reported that the biggest problem we'd be up against was competition for the wheelchair—there were an awful lot of very elderly people there. But all went well, and as I waited for my parents to punch their ballots it occurred to me that the average age of the people then voting around them was clearly above the minimum AARP age. When I mentioned this observation on the way out, my mother replied that elderly people naturally realize they have a lot at stake on election day.

The fact that young people are so much less likely to vote is now so readily apparent that it hardly takes a political scientist to notice it when observing activity at a typical polling place. In the summer of 1998, a Chinese delegation observing a primary election in Georgia expressed amazement that so few people had shown up at the polls, and particularly noted that very few young people had cast ballots. Xu Liugen, the leader of the delegation, summarized his observations to the Associated Press as follows: "I would have some doubts about the representativeness of those who are elected. Why such a low interest? Why don't the young people come to the polls?"[1]

To understand America's current turnout problems, one must answer the questions posed by Xu Liugen. My father's insistence that he really wanted to vote, my casual baby-boomer attitude, and the outright political apathy I frequently see among today's college students are apparently all representative of current generational attitudes toward voting. How, when, and why these generational differences developed are the challenging questions that this chapter seeks to address.

A Comparative Perspective

The phenomenon of relatively low turnout among young people is one that has drawn attention from political analysts in many countries. In 1999 the International Institute for Democracy and Electoral Assistance (IDEA) issued a report showing this problem to be common throughout the democratic world, and described various voter education programs targeted at young people that countries have adopted to try to combat it.[2] The data presented in the IDEA report are less than ideal for the task, however. They are derived from a hodgepodge of studies that differ widely in terms of the time elapsed since the last election, and some refer to a nation's most important election whereas others do not. Fortunately, the Comparative Study of Electoral Systems project now provides an ideal set of comparable national election studies from which generational differences can be assessed.

Unlike the almost unique tendency of Americans with lower degrees of education to be substantially less likely to vote, the United States does not stand out so dramatically in terms of a generation gap in electoral participation. Table 4.1 shows that among the advanced industrialized democracies included in the CSES thus far, Americans under the age of thirty report the second-lowest level of turnout, with only Swiss youth turning out at lower rates. The largest turnout gap between the young and the old is found in Japan, but the United States and Switzerland are not far behind in this respect. Overall, the problem of getting young people to the polls is fairly common. Leaving aside the

Table 4.1   Percentage reporting casting a ballot by age categories in advanced industrialized democracies in recent years

	18–29	30–44	45–64	65+	Difference between under 30 and over 65
Japan	55	82	89	92	−37
United States	53	72	80	84	−31
Switzerland	46	56	75	76	−30
United Kingdom	69	80	88	90	−21
New Zealand[a]	76	83	90	94	−18
Norway	73	85	94	90	−17
Germany	86	92	95	97	−11
Spain	85	90	92	93	−8
Netherlands	88	91	92	94	−6
Australia	98	99	99	100	−2

Source: Comparative Study of Electoral Systems. Validated New Zealand data provided by Jack Vowles.

a. New Zealand data were validated by checking the public records of participation by the respondents.

Australian case, where compulsory election attendance eliminates any substantial turnout rate differences, people under thirty are at least 10 percent less likely to vote in seven out of the nine cases.

It might be thought that young people today, having grown up in an age free of nuclear threats and the cold war, are satisfied with the way that democracy is working and are therefore less concerned about participating than previous generations. The cross-national data do not support this theory, however. Of the ten countries represented in Table 4.1, young people report significantly higher rates of satisfaction with how democracy is working compared with senior citizens in just two—New Zealand and the Netherlands. In three other countries there was no significant difference, and in five countries those under thirty expressed a substantially higher rate of dissatisfaction. Given that the relationship between turnout and dissatisfaction with democracy is not that strong, one shouldn't jump to the conclusion that many young people are abstaining from the electoral process because they are alienated. But the theory that young people are not voting because they are satisfied can be ruled out.

Of course, there is nothing in the CSES data to indicate that declining turnout rates in advanced industrial democracies (see Chapter 1) are due to increasing levels of nonvoting among young people. The simple cross-sectional data shown here could be due to life-cycle and/or generational factors; time-series data would be necessary to sort this out. Thus far such research has been done on Canada and Japan; findings indicate strong generational effects in the decline of turnout in these countries.[3] In the United States a wealth of comparable data over time exists, making it possible to investigate this question in detail.

The Political Know-Nothing Generation

There is little doubt that life-cycle factors play at least some role in explaining the low turnout rates of young people in the United States. National surveys over the last half century have consistently found that electoral participation tends to increase with age. Benjamin Highton and Raymond Wolfinger outline a series of major life changes that young people commonly go through, each of which might make it less likely for them to vote while they sort out their lives.[4] The authors' analysis of the 1996 Census turnout dataset, however, demonstrates that only a small portion of the age differential in turnout can be accounted for by such lifestyle transitions.

A more general reason that may explain some of the steady rise in turnout rates throughout the life cycle is what Donald Green and Ron Shachar call "consuetude." They write that "an act may be said to be subject to consuetude if, other things being equal, merely engaging in the activity today makes it more likely that one will engage in the same activity in the future."[5] Their analysis of the NES panel surveys shows that people are more likely to vote if they have voted in the previous election, even after a host of individual factors that typically predict turnout are controlled for. People who vote regularly learn to feel comfortable with the activity, they argue. And given that American ballots are extraordinarily long and complicated by international standards, this familiarity is likely to be of special importance in the United States. Furthermore, because Americans are asked to vote so often, the process of doing so repeatedly eventually leads to what Green and Scharar describe as an attitude that going to the polls is "what people like me do on election day." The story at the outset of this chapter about my father insisting on voting reflects just such an attitude; obviously young people need time to develop this feeling.

The problems of youth turnout in America today, however, go well beyond the normal life-cycle factors. An analyst looking at the various data from 1972, when eighteen- to twenty-one-year-olds were first enfranchised, could have reasonably concluded that young people were interested in politics, but many just had not yet gotten around to clearing the registration hurdles and getting into the habit of voting. Today the stereotype of politically apathetic youth is so widespread that politicians are even discussing it openly. For example, before his historic return to space, Senator John Glenn remarked that he worried "about the future when we have so many young people who feel apathetic and critical and cynical about anything having to do with politics. They don't want to touch it. And yet politics is literally the personnel system for democracy."[6] Similarly, when Al Gore appeared on MTV during the 2000 presidential campaign, he said,

"There are a lot of young people who have kind of stayed away from the political process. There is a lot of disillusionment. Try to fight through that."[7]

Stereotypes can be found to be mistaken; unfortunately this is one case where widely held impressions are overwhelmingly supported by solid evidence, which will be reviewed briefly here. It is important to note that this is not to say that young people are inactive in American society. Nearly three of four college freshmen surveyed in 1998 reported volunteering for a community group during their senior year in high school. It is only when it comes to politics that young people seem to express indifference about getting involved. Whether because they feel they can't make a difference, believe the political system to be corrupt, or just have not received any exposure to politics, young Americans are clearly apathetic about public affairs. And while political apathy isn't restricted to young people, a tremendous gap has opened up between the young and the elderly on measures of political interest, media consumption about politics, political knowledge, and, of course, turnout.

The high level of political apathy among young people today is unexpected given that their educational achievement levels are so high. Even those who have made it into college are expressing remarkably little concern for politics. A yearly nationwide study of college freshmen recently found that among the class of 2002 only 26 percent said that "keeping up with politics" was an important priority for them, compared with 58 percent among the class of 1970—their parents' generation.[8] If one looks more broadly at all people under the age of thirty, the NES data on "following what's going on in government and public affairs" display a striking decline in political attentiveness among young people since 1964. Table 4.2 shows that from 1964 through 1976 there was little difference between those under thirty and those over sixty-five in terms of this measure of general political interest,

Table 4.2   General interest in public affairs in the United States by age, 1964–2000

	18–29	30–44	45–64	65+	Difference between under 30 and over 65
1964	56	67	64	63	−7
1968	58	60	63	53	+5
1972	65	68	67	62	+3
1976	58	67	70	65	−7
1980	48	56	62	64	−16
1984	50	57	62	64	−14
1988	46	54	58	63	−17
1992	53	60	65	65	−12
1996	45	51	64	64	−19
2000	38	50	60	64	−26

Source: National Election Studies.
Note: The four response categories have been recoded as follows: hardly at all = 0; only now and then = 33; some of the time = 66; most of the time = 100.

with young people actually showing a bit more interest in 1968 and 1972. Since 1980, however, the youngest voting-age citizens have consistently expressed the least interest in public affairs by a substantial margin. The 2000 survey findings, in particular, mark a new low in political interest among young people. Only 33 percent of respondents under thirty said they followed government and public affairs most or some of the time; among senior citizens, the figure was 73 percent. As expected, campaign interest was also at a new low for young people in 2000—only 11 percent said they were very interested in the campaign as opposed to 39 percent among the elderly.

Why young people today are not interested in public affairs is a difficult question to answer. Since I started asking my students for their opinion on this nearly a decade ago, I have gotten more possible answers than I ever could have dreamed of. Typically, the first response I get is something to the effect that politics just

hasn't affected their generation the way it did previous generations. Certainly, today's youth have not had any policy touch
their lives the way the draft and the Vietnam War affected their
parents, or the way Medicare has benefited their grandparents.
Mark Gray and I asked a question regarding people's perceptions
of this in our post-2000 election survey of four southern California counties. The question went as follows: "Some of the issues
discussed during the campaigns for the November election directly related to policies affecting people of your generation. Do
you think that politicians pay too much attention to these issues,
about the right amount or too little?" Sixty-two percent of respondents under the age of thirty said "too little," 21 percent said
"about the right amount," and 9 percent said "too much." The
percentages for those sixty-five and over were 33, 41, and 11 percent, respectively.

However, I believe that the cause of young people's apathy runs
much deeper than a sense that the issues aren't relevant to them
and that the politicians ignore them. Central to any generational
hypothesis are changes in socialization experiences. For the last
two decades, young people have been socialized in a rapidly
changing media environment that has been radically different
from that experienced by the past couple of generations. Political
scientists were slow to realize the impact of television—as late as
1980 there was surprisingly little literature on this subject. Today
a similar shortcoming is the lack of research concerning how the
shift from broadcasting to narrowcasting has dramatically altered
how much exposure a young adult has received to politics while
growing up. The first major networks—ABC, NBC, and CBS—
chose to use the term "broadcasting" in the names of their companies because their signal was being sent out to a broad audience. As long as these networks dominated the industry, each
would have to deal with general topics that the public as a whole
was concerned with, such as politics and government. But with

the development of cable television, market segmentation has taken hold. Sports buffs can watch ESPN all day, music buffs can tune to MTV or VH1, history buffs can go to the History Channel, and so forth. Rather than appealing to a general audience, channels such as ESPN, MTV, and C-SPAN focus on a narrow particular interest. Hence their mission has often been termed "narrowcasting," rather than the traditional "broadcasting." This is even more true for Web sites, which require far less in start-up costs than a television channel and hence can be successful with a very small and specific audience.

Because of the narrowcasting revolution, today's youth have grown up in an environment in which public affairs news has not been as readily visible as it has been in the past. It has become particularly difficult to convince members of a generation that has channel surfed all their lives that politics really does matter. Major political events were once shared national experiences. The current generation of young adults is the first to grow up in a media environment in which there are few such shared experiences. When CBS, NBC, and ABC dominated the airwaves, their blanket coverage of presidential speeches, political conventions, and presidential debates sometimes left little else to watch on television. As channels have proliferated over the last two decades, though, it has become much easier to avoid exposure to politics altogether by simply grabbing the remote control. Whereas President Nixon got an average rating of 50 for his televised addresses to the nation (meaning that half the population was watching), President Clinton averaged only about 30 in his first term.[9] Political conventions, which once received more television coverage than the Summer Olympics, have been relegated to an hour per night, and even this highly condensed coverage gets poor ratings. The presidential debates of 1996 and 2000 drew respectable average ratings of 28, but this was only half the typical level of viewers drawn by debates held between 1960 and

Table 4.3 Percentage reading newspapers about the campaign by age, 1960–2000

	18–29	30–44	45–64	65+	Difference between under 30 and over 65
1960	84	80	81	74	+10
1964	75	80	80	77	−2
1968	68	81	76	72	−4
1972	49	59	62	61	−11
1976	68	78	77	70	−2
1980	56	78	76	72	−16
1984	62	77	77	70	−8
1988[a]	35	47	57	57	−22
1992	35	50	57	60	−25
1996	28	39	52	60	−32
2000	27	35	48	56	−29

Source: National Election Studies.
a. Major change in question format occurred here.

1980. In sum, young people today have never known a time when most citizens paid attention to major political events. This is one of the key reasons why so many of them have yet to get into the habit of following and participating in politics.

More specifically, one key media consumption habit that young people have not developed is reading the daily newspaper. As Teixeria shows, newspaper reading is particularly predictive of who votes, even after controlling for a host of demographic and attitudinal variables.[10] Table 4.3 displays percentages of people reading campaign stories in the newspaper since 1960 by age group. From 1960 to 1976, there was no consistent difference in this measure between the youngest and oldest citizens. Since 1980, though, those under thirty have been substantially less likely to pick up a newspaper and read about the presidential race. In both 1996 and 2000, senior citizens were more than twice as likely to say they had read campaign articles in newspapers as those under thirty.

Because of the media environment that young people have been socialized in, they have learned much less about politics than their elders. The current pattern of political knowledge increasing with age has become well known in recent years. But it was not always that way. The 1964 and 2000 National Election Studies each contain a substantial battery of political knowledge questions that enable this point to be demonstrated. Figure 4.1 shows the percentage of correct answers to eight questions in 1964 and nine questions in 2000 by age category.[11] In 1964 there was virtually no pattern by age, with those under thirty actually scoring 5 percent higher on this test than senior citizens. By contrast, in 2000 young people provided the correct answer to only one out of every three questions, whereas people over sixty-five were correct half the time. Regardless of whether the question concerned identifying current political leaders, information about the presidential candidates, or partisan control of the Congress, the result was the same: young people were less knowledgeable than the elderly.

Given that today's youth has not been exposed to politics through the broadcasting of national shared experiences, the label of the "know-nothing generation" ought to be considered descriptive, not pejorative. It is not their fault. But nevertheless the consequences are real and important. Thomas Jefferson once said that there has never been, nor ever will be, a people who are politically ignorant and free. If this is indeed the case, write Stephen Bennett and Eric Rademacher, then "we can legitimately wonder what the future holds if Xers remain as uninformed as they are about government and public affairs."[12] Although this worry may well be an overreaction, important consequences ensue when citizens lack political information. In *What Americans Know about Politics and Why It Matters*, Michael Delli Carpini and Scott Keeter

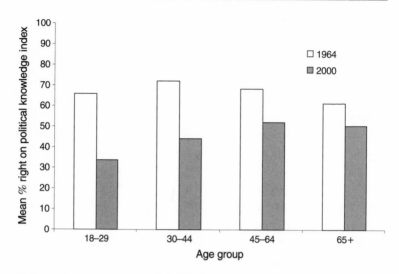

Figure 4.1 Age and political knowledge: 1964 and 2000 compared. Entries are based on the percentage of accurate responses to a series of eight questions in 1964 and nine questions in 2000. In 1964, respondents were given credit for knowing that Goldwater was from Arizona, Johnson was from Texas, Goldwater and Johnson were Protestants, Democrats had the majority in Congress both before and after the election, Johnson had supported civil rights legislation, and Goldwater had opposed it. In 2000, respondents were given credit for knowing that Bush was from Texas, Gore was from Tennessee, Republicans had the majority in the House and Senate before the election, Lieberman was Jewish, and for identifying William Rehnquist, Tony Blair, Janet Reno, and Trent Lott. (Data from National Election Studies, 1964 and 2000.)

make a strong case for the importance of staying informed about public affairs. Political knowledge, they argue: (1) fosters civic virtues, such as political tolerance; (2) helps citizens to identify what policies would truly benefit them and to incorporate this information in their voting behavior; and (3) promotes active participation in politics.[13] It is certainly the case that lacking information about politics in comparison with their elders, fewer young

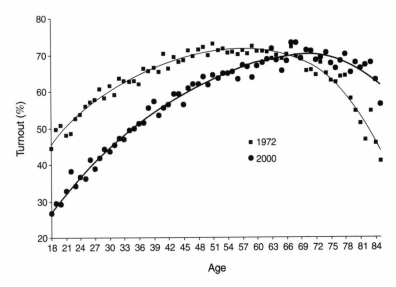

Figure 4.2 Age and turnout in presidential elections: 1972 and 2000 compared. (Data from U.S. Census Bureau studies.)

Americans are heading to the polls compared with previous generations—a development that has pulled the nationwide turnout rate down substantially in recent years.

The Age-Turnout Relationship over Time and in Different Types of Elections

The standard source for information on the precise relationship between age and turnout in the United States has long been Wolfinger and Rosenstone's graph in *Who Votes?*, based on 1972 data.[14] This curve is displayed somewhat more precisely in Figure 4.2, along with comparable data from the 2000 Census survey. There have been several striking changes in the age-turnout pattern. The data for ages 18 to 60 show a noticeable decline in turnout from 1972 to 2000; importantly, the rate of decline increases as one moves downward in age. In contrast, it is readily apparent that turnout has actually gone up for ages sixty-eight and above. Political scientists used to write that the frailties of old age led to a decline in turnout after one became eligible for Social Security; now an examination of the Census survey data shows that such a decline occurs only after eighty years of age. The greater access to medical care provided to today's seniors must surely be given some of the credit for this change. Because senior citizens personally benefit from government programs like Medicare, it is particularly easy for them to believe that politics does indeed make a difference.

The available data from the 1974 and 1998 midterm elections do not show quite as dramatic a change in the age-turnout relationship, but the findings from presidential elections are largely confirmed. Figure 4.3 shows that turnout decline has been less among younger people in midterm than in presidential years. This finding is probably due to the fact that youth turnout in midterms was already so low by 1974 that it could hardly fall by much. The turnout rates of elderly people, however, had more room to rise, and this can in fact be seen for all age groups above sixty. Overall, the elderly now have even greater clout in midterm than in presidential elections. Because young people tend to be peripheral voters who have not gotten into the habit of going to the polls regularly, it should not be surprising to find an extremely wide generation gap in turnout for low-salience contests like midterms.

This phenomenon can also be seen in public records of turnout rates by age in primaries and special elections. Table 4.4 presents data on such elections from a variety of U.S. localities that have posted such information on the Internet. These percentages are based on registered voters only, because the local election officials

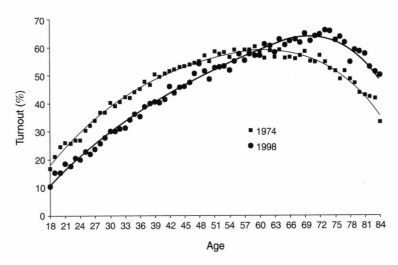

Figure 4.3 Age and turnout in midterm elections: 1974 and 1998 compared. (Data from U.S. Census Bureau studies.)

who compiled the data are strictly interested in who on their registration rolls has turned out. If one were to take into account the lower registration rates of young people, then the generational differences would be even greater.[15] The results just for registered voters, however, are disturbing enough. Young registrants, being more likely to be Independents, rarely participate in primaries. Their single-digit primary participation is dwarfed by margins ranging from 4:1 to 12:1 in the localities shown in Table 4.4. Young people are thus taking a very small part in the choosing of party nominees. The situation with regard to special elections held to decide referenda questions does not seem to be quite as bad. Nevertheless, it is clear that separating such policy decisions from high-salience elections gives extra weight to the opinions of the elderly, who are much more likely to turn out in such circumstances.

Table 4.4 Turnout percentages among registered voters by age in special elections and primaries for various counties and states

Age	Pierce County, Wash., 1999 referendum election	Age	Alaska, 1999 referendum election	Age	Johnson County, Kans., 2000 primary
18–25	26.3	18–24	22.3	18–24	3.2
26–35	40.2	25–34	27.9	25–39	15.0
36–50	60.4	35–54	45.4	40–59	44.8
51–65	76.8	55–64	56.3	60+	37.0
66+	81.4	65+	61.8		

Age	Brevard County, Fla., first 1998 primary	Age	Tri-County, Ore., 1998 primary	Age	South Carolina, 2000 primary
18–29	5.5	18–29	10.0	18–21	8.8
30–39	13.8	30–39	19.0	22–44	11.0
40–49	19.3	40–49	32.9	45–64	23.9
50–59	24.0	50–59	44.2	65+	31.1
60–69	29.7	60–69	58.8		
70–79	30.5	70–79	66.0		
80+	23.6				

Why Low Youth Turnout Matters

Although many young people seem to think it doesn't matter if they don't vote, it does. Harold Lasswell wrote many years ago that "politics is who gets what, when, and how." As long as young people have low rates of participation in the electoral process, then they should expect to be getting relatively little of whatever there is to get from government. Yet until they start showing up in greater numbers at the polls, there will be little incentive for politicians to focus on programs that will help them. Politicians are not fools; they know who their customers are. Why should they worry about young nonvoters any more than the makers of denture cream worry about people with healthy teeth?

If one had to choose a single word to describe the relationship between candidates for office and young citizens it would probably have to be "neglect." This was the starting premise for a multidimensional study of young adults during the 2000 presidential campaign aptly titled "Neglection 2000."[16] One of the most interesting findings to come out of this study stemmed from an analysis of the placement of political commercials during the primary and general election seasons. Using Nielsen demographic data for the shows where the ads ran, the principal investigators produced a measurement of political ad impressions by multiplying each ad by the age distribution for the program. They found that the candidates overwhelmingly chose to place ads on shows with older audiences, such as "Jeopardy" or "Wheel of Fortune," and avoided ads on shows like syndicated reruns of "Friends," which draws a young audience. All told, in a selection of key media markets during the general election campaign, they found that political ads were shown to audiences in which 64 percent of the people were over fifty, as opposed to just 14 percent for people under thirty-five. The steeper age gradient in primary participation might lead candidates to focus even more on older audiences. But given the intensity with which presidential primaries move from state to state, campaigns sometimes have to pick up ads wherever they can get them. In a selection of key primary media markets, nevertheless, the Neglection 2000 project found that 58 percent of ad impressions reached people over fifty versus just 17 percent for those under thirty-five.

The authors of the Neglection 2000 study quite properly conclude that "the result of these trends in ad purchasing is an uninformed segment of the population."[17] Although some older voters might envy younger adults for their lack of exposure to political ads, especially harsh negative ones, studies have consistently shown that people learn from political ads—both positive and negative.[18] Furthermore, because political ads both shape and represent much of the agenda of any modern campaign, it is readily apparent that the concerns of young people are likely to be ignored. Rather than addressing their ads to programs that young people are likely to be particularly interested in, such as job training programs, candidates are much more apt to be discussing policy questions concerning health care and retirement. Such a focus is likely to perpetuate, and perhaps even exacerbate, the current age bias in electoral participation.

Of course, most everyone can look forward to getting older eventually. Those who were neglected in the 2000 presidential campaign will probably be seriously courted in the campaign of 2040. From this perspective, it could be argued that most people will one day get the chance to be heard in the electoral process and to reap the political benefits. Such a perspective, however, assumes that there are not generational differences in attitudes that can influence the course of public policy. Who gets what does not just involve material goods, but has also been increasingly about basic nonmaterial values in recent years. Ronald Inglehart has documented a shift from materialist to postmaterialist values throughout the advanced industrialized world, which has been largely driven by generational change and replacement.[19]

There are indeed sharp differences between younger and older Americans on both material and nonmaterial issue questions, as displayed in Table 4.5. In order to have plenty of cases for analysis, data from the 1992 through 1998 National Election Studies were combined, yielding 1,526 respondents under the age of thirty and 1,252 respondents who were at least sixty-five. As expected, young people are substantially more supportive of government spending that would particularly help them, such as for public schools and jobs programs. Roughly similar differences in terms of magnitude can also be found for value questions. Young

Table 4.5   Young vs. elderly opinion on the issues in the 1990s (in percent)

	Under 30	65 and over
Liberal	23	11
Moderate	25	28
Conservative	26	31
Don't know	27	29
Favor govt. help to get people jobs	35	19
In-between	19	23
People must get ahead on their own	35	43
Don't know	11	16
Favor more govt. spending for things like education and health care	39	21
In-between	22	30
Prefer less domestic spending	23	30
Don't know	16	19
Favor increased spending for public schools	80	54
Same	17	41
Want decreased school spending	3	6
Favor increased spending to protect the environment	61	41
Same	34	53
Want decreased environmental spending	5	6
Favor equal role for women	67	44
In-between	15	20
Women's place is in the home	14	25
Don't know	4	12
Never permit abortion	11	14
OK for rape, incest, health	28	34
OK for other reasons	15	14
Abortion should be a matter of personal choice	45	36
Don't know	1	3

Source: Combined data from the 1992–1998 National Election Studies.

people are more in favor of spending to protect the environment, an equal role for women in society, and abortion rights. In terms of general ideological labeling, young people are virtually as likely to say they are liberals as conservatives on the ideological scale, whereas among senior citizens conservatives outnumber liberals by 20 percent. In sum, if young people had turnout rates equal to those of older people, voting behavior and public policy would probably be shifted noticeably to the left.

Conclusion

It is not young people's fault that they have not been exposed much to politics while growing up and hence are less informed about politics than previous generations. Their low turnout rates are understandable in light of their unique socialization experience.

American politicians are not really to blame for this inequitable pattern of generational representation, either. They didn't consciously try to create a situation that would greatly benefit older people. It is only natural for them to study who has voted in the past and to focus on these people, thereby leaving most young adults out of the picture. But if politicians were to ponder the principles universally valued in any democracy they might be moved to address this problem. If official election observers in a third world country noticed that older people were three times as likely as younger people to vote, they would no doubt call this fact to the attention of local authorities and suggest there was an imbalance that ought to be looked into. As former president Jimmy Carter remarked at a hearing of the 2001 National Commission on Federal Election Reform, "This [issue of young people not voting] is something that is just as bad as the difference in ethnic groups or minorities not voting."[20]

A well-established democracy like the United States ironically has fewer options than a third world country for dealing with such a problem. In a new democracy, for example, it would be easier to change the electoral system to facilitate the emergence of a party that would particularly appeal to young people. It seems unlikely, however, that there will ever be any serious consideration of changing the single-member district system in the United States. A strong independent candidacy, such as that of Ross Perot in 1992, may emerge from time to time to energize young people a bit, but an enduring viable third party is nowhere on the horizon. Of course, nothing precludes one of the existing two major parties from targeting this large bloc of unmobilized young adults. Given young people's opinions on policy questions, however, there is little reason to expect the Republicans to do so. And the Democrats, having spent decades building up their image as creators and protectors of Social Security and Medicare, would find it difficult to switch gears and try to make themselves the party of the young.

It would theoretically be easier to make additions to the modern television campaign so that everyone, especially young people, would be more likely to be exposed to the discussion of the issues. In 1992 the presidential candidates were suddenly everywhere on the television dial, appearing on MTV, the Nashville Network, the "Arsenio Hall Show," and many forums. Voters seemed to like the idea of candidates cutting through the journalistic filters and talking to them on programs they regularly watched. This election marked the only one in the time period under consideration in this book when turnout went up substantially, a pattern that was especially evident among young people. Such broad-based exposure for the candidates needs to be somehow institutionalized for the narrowcasting age. (One proposal to do this will be discussed in Chapter 7.)

Although the solution to the new generation gap in voting participation in the United States is going to be difficult to find, the consequences for the present are readily apparent. Major issues that affect young adults are not even making it onto the public agenda, and young people's opinions on the issues are not being faithfully represented through the political process. Who votes does matter, as the next chapter will show in greater depth.

Who Votes Does Make a Difference

Implicit in past as well as present political battles over election reform has been the premise that who votes has an impact on results at the polls. Yet the most widely cited academic studies employing survey data all come to the conclusion that there is little difference between voters and nonvoters in terms of political behavior. If these studies are right, then despite having one of the lowest turnout rates in the advanced industrialized world, Americans need not be concerned about an unrepresentative electorate deciding who governs.

Three of the most widely read books on turnout and participation in recent years all reach the conclusion that nonvoting does not produce an unrepresentative electorate in presidential elections. Wolfinger and Rosenstone's classic book *Who Votes?* demonstrates that nonvoters are demographically different than voters, but argues that "these demographic biases do not translate into discernible overrepresentation of particular policy constituencies."[1] The lack of policy differences between voters and nonvoters leads Wolfinger and Rosenstone to conclude that turnout rates do not influence election outcomes.

Teixeira's superb work on turnout decline asks the question "What if they gave an election and everybody came?" and arrives at an answer of "Not much."[2] He too places much weight on the finding that demographic factors are not closely enough related to policy preferences to result in substantial differences in the political attitudes of voters and nonvoters. Indeed, Teixeira's analysis of the 1988 NES reveals the same pattern that Wolfinger and Rosenstone found with the 1972 NES. Furthermore, his analysis of whom nonvoters said they would have voted for in various presidential elections reveals that their preferences have closely paralleled those of voters.

Most recently, Sidney Verba, Kay Lehman Schlozman, and Henry Brady's comprehensive review of participation in the United States updates Wolfinger and Rosenstone's analysis by examining how people who regularly vote in presidential elections (as ascertained in 1987) compare with the population on the issues of jobs and government services. They write, "Our data support the conclusion that voters and non-voters do not seem to differ substantially in their attitudes on public policy issues."[3]

The extraordinary closeness of the 2000 presidential election surely casts doubt on such conclusions. A variety of small changes in group turnout rates could have easily swung the outcome in Gore's favor. But one need not rely on evidence from a presidential election to establish that who votes really matters. Indeed, one of the major problems with the current literature on turnout is that it has been far too focused on elections for just this one office. Any conclusions regarding turnout bias based solely on analyzing presidential elections risk overgeneralizing from the least typical of all American elections. The majority of electoral choices are made not on the day every four years when presidents are selected, but instead at times when turnout is invariably lower. In elections with substantially lower turnout, such as midterm elections, special elections, and primaries, the chances are greater that evidence of important turnout bias will be found. This is a simple extension of the basic principle of sampling: the bigger the percentage of the population that participates, the more likely the results will reflect what would be found if everyone were included.

This chapter will first review a variety of evidence concerning how turnout influenced the 2000 presidential election. It will then turn to a case study of the 1994 midterm election, which was arguably one of the most important in recent times, establishing the first Republican-controlled Congress in forty years. The 1994 midterms provide just one of many possible examples of turnout biases in elections with relatively low participation rates.

Turnout Bias and the 2000 Presidential Election

One of the most frequently discussed aspects of the 2000 presidential election has been the fact that George W. Bush lost the popular vote but won in the Electoral College—the first time this had happened in an American presidential election since 1888. In the view of many, his election was tainted in that he did not have the support of more voters than Al Gore. Most knowledgeable observers are aware of the small-state advantage in the Electoral College that favored Bush, who won a disproportionate share of the small states that are overrepresented by this system. But few have recognized the fact that differences in state turnout rates disadvantaged Bush in the popular vote totals nationwide. It doesn't really matter for practical purposes whether a state has a high or low turnout rate, because its electoral votes will be allocated to the winner in either event. However, it does matter in terms of rolling up a margin in the popular vote. Had the Constitution called for the national popular vote to decide the presidency, the Bush campaign would surely have devoted considerable effort to getting a higher turnout in states where they were very strong and turnout has typically been low, such as Texas.

They naturally didn't do so under the circumstances, and as can be seen in Table 5.1, it just so happened that the states with the lowest turnout rates most favored Bush over Gore.

What if all states had experienced an identical turnout rate and the percentage of voters for each candidate in each state remained unchanged? The answer is that Bush would have won the popular vote by the very slimmest of margins. Rather than the actual 0.51 percent margin by which Gore won the popular vote, equalizing state turnout rates yields a popular vote margin of 0.00076 percent for Bush. Thus it can be said that a major reason that Bush won the presidency without winning the popular vote is that his best states had very poor turnout rates. Such a finding is merely academic, being heavily dependent on various assumptions, but it does shed a different light on how to interpret the 2000 presidential election.

The assumption that is most questionable in the above analysis is that a state's turnout rate can change without altering the percentage of the vote for each candidate. Indeed, the major point of this chapter is that changing who votes can often determine the results enough to affect the outcome. The Florida 2000 vote provides an easy demonstration of this point, from the perspective both of how Gore was disadvantaged by low turnout among one group (young people) and of how Bush was advantaged by high turnout among another (Miami's Hispanic Republicans).

George W. Bush and Al Gore each devoted substantial effort to winning the support of Florida's elderly voters. They did so in part due to the well-known fact that senior citizens are particularly numerous in Florida. But strategists for both campaigns were probably also aware of the fact that the turnout gap between young and old people is typically quite high in the Sunshine State. The 2000 Census survey found that Floridians who were at least sixty years of age voted at a 69 percent rate compared with a 33 percent rate for those under thirty. According to the 2000

Table 5.1   Presidential vote in 2000 by state turnout rate (in percent)

Turnout of citizens	Bush	Gore	Nader	Others
Less than 50%	55.6	41.8	1.5	1.0
Between 50% and 55%	47.7	48.7	2.6	1.0
Between 55% and 60%	45.3	51.4	2.5	0.9
Over 60%	45.0	48.9	4.8	1.3

Source: Calculated by the author from official election returns and U.S. Census Bureau estimates of each state's number of citizens of voting age.

Florida exit poll, people under thirty who did go to the polls supported Gore over Bush by a margin of 55 to 40 percent. In contrast, the much more numerous group of Florida voters over sixty favored Bush over Gore by 51 to 47 percent. Given the closeness of the outcome, it is obvious that had turnout rates among young people been just slightly higher, Gore would have carried the state and hence won the White House. Equalizing turnout rates among the generations increases Gore's share of the two-party vote in Florida by about 0.8 percent.[4]

Whereas the failure to mobilize young people in Florida was critical to Gore's defeat, success in mobilizing Miami's registered Hispanic Republicans was key to Bush's victory. For weeks the nation was gripped in suspense over the battle of whether or not to recount Miami-Dade County's ballots, or at least its presidential undervotes, by hand. The *Miami Herald* put out a regular series entitled "The Florida Count: What Went Wrong," which continued to examine minutiae about the election for months after the outcome was settled.[5] Lost in this flurry of news coverage concerning problems with the election process, however, was an important story from Miami regarding what went right. Any time a group exhibits a very high turnout rate, the story is a positive one, given that the expression of opinions through ballots is what democracy is all about. Furthermore, when such a group

Table 5.2 Turnout percentages by racial category in Miami-Dade County in 2000. (Numbers in parentheses are actual number of voters registered.)

	Whites	Blacks	Hispanics	Other race
Democrats	74.5 (137,109)	72.6 (154,766)	67.9 (95,286)	64.8 (15,384)
Republicans	71.6 (96,405)	57.7 (7,473)	*79.5* (227,617)	70.7 (10,681)
Nonpartisans	62.1 (50,325)	56.0 (18,111)	64.0 (80,429)	59.6 (15,790)

Source: Data made available by Miami-Dade County supervisor of elections.
Note: Italic indicates highest percentage of any racial-party combination in Miami.

overwhelmingly favors one candidate over the other in an extremely tight election, there is little doubt that its participation has been crucial in determining the outcome. This scenario is readily apparent for Miami's Hispanics who were registered as Republicans in 2000. Table 5.2 shows that their turnout rate of 79.5 percent was the highest for any racial-party combination in Miami. Assuming that Miami's Hispanic Republicans favored Bush over Gore by about eight to one, as did Republicans nationwide, it can be estimated that had their turnout rate in Miami been equal to that of Hispanic Democrats that Bush would have garnered approximately 20,500 fewer votes. Or, had their turnout rate merely fallen to the level of the next highest group—White Democrats—Bush would have gained 8,900 less votes. In either event, the highly successful mobilization of Miami's Hispanic Republicans gave Bush far more votes than were ever disputed during the national trauma over the Florida 2000 vote.

The extraordinary closeness of the 2000 presidential election has made it fairly easy to identify examples that demonstrate that who votes matters. Yet it may well be that no one who lived through it will ever again see a presidential election nearly that close (though it should be noted that such statements were also made after the 1960 campaign). In contrast, close contests for control of the House of Representatives have become the norm in recent years. Partisan control of the House was decided by 13 seats or less out of the total of 435 in each of the four elections from 1994 to 2000. Although most House races are not very competitive these days, partisan control of the House could easily have turned on who voted in the closest districts. The following case study of the 1994 elections provides evidence for just such a scenario.

A Case Study of the 1994 Midterm Elections

The 1994 midterms were an important historical turning point. The new Republican majorities in the House and Senate, dashed any hopes among liberals for enacting new programs such as national health care during the remainder of the Clinton presidency. Soon afterward, President Clinton himself proclaimed to a joint session of Congress that "the era of big government is over." And indeed it was.

During the early days of the 104th Congress, when the House was rushing to pass the bills embodied in the "Contract with America," I happened to see a bumper sticker that read "Newt happens when only 37 percent of Americans vote." Besides expressing the popularly held perception that turnout matters, this slogan poses an important research question: would Gingrich and the Republicans still have won the majority of House seats if turnout had been greater?

A simple way to address this question is to assess the difference it would have made if voters had mirrored the adult population in terms of education. As shown in Table 5.3, 30 percent of 1994 voters who lacked a high school diploma voted for GOP House candidates, compared with 62 percent of voters with college de-

Table 5.3   Turnout bias by education in 1994 and its consequences

	Percentage of population	Percentage of voters	Percentage voting Republican for the House
Less than high school	18.6	10.7	29.7
High school diploma	34.1	30.8	49.6
Some college	26.5	29.1	52.1
College degree	14.1	19.0	63.8
Advanced degree	6.6	10.4	60.1

If turnout rates match the Census Bureau findings, then the national Republican vote = 52.0%.

If turnout rates are representative, then the national Republican vote = 49.2%.

Sources: 1994 Census Bureau study for columns 1 and 2; 1994 National Election Study for column 3.

grees. Therefore, just increasing the turnout rate of the least educated citizens would surely have made some difference. Overall, it can be calculated from the information in Table 5.3 that if turnout rates had been equal among all education categories, the Republican share of the vote would have fallen from 52.0 to 49.2 percent.

Although it is unlikely that Americans of differing education levels would ever vote at exactly the same rate, this is only one of many biases in electoral participation. A more comprehensive method of estimating the impact of higher turnout is to gauge the likely behavior of the nonvoters who could have most easily been mobilized—those who were already on the registration lists. As Angus Campbell argued decades ago, people who drop out of the electorate during a low-stimulus election differ from nonvoters in a presidential election.[6] Presidential elections motivate a good percentage of registered citizens to come to the polls; in other elections, many who are registered do not vote. Compared with the politically uninterested nonregistrants, registered nonvoters are far more likely to have their political behavior influenced by short-term political forces. If these demobilized individuals are reacting to the political environment by sitting out a particular election, their nonparticipation may well create a bias at the polls.

Table 5.4 demonstrates that registered nonvoters in 1994 were consistently more pro-Democratic than were voters on a variety of measures of partisanship. Among voters, 49 percent either identified as Republicans or leaned toward them compared with 44 percent for the Democrats; for registered nonvoters the figures were 35 percent Republican to 55 percent Democratic. Furthermore, the turnout bias extends beyond the long-term attitude of party identification to short-term evaluations of the parties in 1994. Registered nonvoters were about evenly split regarding which party would best handle the problem they judged most important, whereas those who voted picked the Republicans by more than two to one. Registered nonvoters rated the Democratic Party four points higher on average on the feeling-thermometer scale than the Republican Party; voters preferred the Republicans by an average of five points. When registered citizens were asked what they liked and disliked about the two parties, those who voted were more likely to offer positive comments about the Republicans and negative comments about the Democrats.

It should be emphasized that the above findings regarding turnout bias would be obscured if one were to combine all nonvoters, as is commonly done in such analyses. Although unregistered individuals were more likely to label themselves Democrats than Republicans, on the three short-term measures they leaned more toward the GOP. Thus a simple comparison of voters and nonvoters would find much less of a partisan bias than the focus here on only registered individuals reveals. Because registered re-

Table 5.4 Partisan attitudes in 1994 by registration and turnout (in percent, except for feeling thermometer ratings)

	Voters	Registered but did not vote	Not registered
Party identification			
Strong Democrat	18	13	7
Weak Democrat	16	24	20
Independent Democrat	10	18	17
Pure Independent	7	11	18
Independent Republican	14	8	11
Weak Republican	14	16	17
Strong Republican	21	11	7
Apolitical	0	1	3
Party best on most important problem			
Democrats	16	19	12
No difference, don't know	48	60	70
Republicans	36	21	19
Mean feeling thermometer score			
Democratic Party	53	58	55
Republican Party	58	54	56
Percentage positive on open-ended comments about:			
Democratic Party	42	50	42
Republican Party	52	47	50

Source: 1994 National Election Study.

spondents who sat out a congressional election are far more likely to vote in presidential elections than those who are unregistered, this distinction is crucial in assessing the impact of the turnout differential between high- and low-stimulus elections.

The practical implication stemming from the findings presented thus far is that Clinton could have designed his reelection strategy with the expectation that he would benefit from the inevitable increase in turnout from 1994 to 1996. This point can be

Table 5.5 Evaluations of Clinton in 1994 by registration and turnout (in percent, except for feeling thermometer rating)

	Voters	Registered but did not vote	Not registered
Presidential approval			
Strongly approve	18	20	24
Approve	30	35	32
Disapprove	16	22	23
Strongly disapprove	35	23	21
Average feeling thermometer rating			
of Clinton	52	58	57
Leader preference			
Prefer Clinton	47	61	55
Rate both equally	8	14	13
Prefer Dole	45	25	32

Source: 1994 National Election Study.

demonstrated most clearly using the data in Table 5.5 examining evaluations of Clinton according to turnout and registration status in 1994. In line with Samuel Kernell's earlier findings, those who approved of the president's performance in office were less likely to vote in the midterm election.[7] Most noteworthy, however, is that a full 61 percent of registered nonvoters preferred Clinton over Dole on feeling-thermometer ratings compared with only 24 percent who rated Dole higher than Clinton. In contrast, 1994 voters split almost evenly in terms of preference for Clinton versus Dole. Thus an exit poll from 1994 might lead an analyst to project a very close presidential race, whereas taking into account the pro-Clinton leanings of registered citizens who stayed home in 1994 would lead to a more favorable projection for President Clinton. It certainly seems that Republican congressional leaders, in their glee over the 1994 results, misinterpreted them by not taking turnout bias into consideration.

Because the 1994 congressional election was interpreted by some analysts as a mandate for the "Contract with America" and the goal of reducing the scope of government, the question of a turnout bias with respect to policy issues takes on special significance. The data displayed in Table 5.6 demonstrate that conservative laissez-faire principles were far more evident among voters than among nonvoters in 1994. Unlike the findings regarding partisanship and candidate evaluations, unregistered respondents are found to be even more liberal on policy questions than registered nonvoters. This is particularly the case with respect to the economic issues of government health insurance and job programs.

It is probably more than coincidental that Clinton's two most visible policy failures—the 1994 effort to establish universal health care and the 1993 economic stimulus package—had their strongest support from unregistered citizens who are the least likely to ever vote. Republicans in the 103rd Congress may thus have rationally anticipated that the strongest constituencies for these Clinton proposals were unlikely to judge them in 1994. In the 104th Congress, in contrast, Republicans should have anticipated that their budget-cutting proposals would receive less support from an expanded set of voters in 1996. Whereas the credit for Clinton's comeback in 1996 is often given to the triangulation strategy designed by his pollster Dick Morris, these results suggest that another plausible factor was the increase in turnout from 1994 and 1996.

There are two principal ways we can assess how nonvoters in 1994 would have cast their ballots had they turned out. The most direct method is to examine which House candidate they preferred on a feeling thermometer. Only about a fifth of nonvoters (registered or unregistered) were able to rate both major-party candidates for the House of Representatives, but these are presumably the most likely people to vote in a higher-stimulus elec-

Table 5.6 Issue preferences in 1994 by registration and turnout (in percent)

	Voters	Registered but did not vote	Not registered
Ideology			
Liberal	10	11	11
Slightly liberal	10	9	9
Moderate	29	41	41
Slightly conservative	18	19	20
Conservative	33	19	20
Government services			
Favor more	26	37	39
In-between	26	26	33
Favor less	48	37	28
Health insurance			
Government plan	33	41	49
In-between	22	21	21
Private plans	45	38	31
Jobs programs			
Government should help	24	34	39
In-between	24	22	27
People help selves	52	44	34
Aid to Blacks			
Government should help	20	22	21
In-between	24	22	27
People help selves	54	53	53
Abortion			
Women's choice	45	44	38
Clear need	14	17	16
Rape/incest/health	30	28	32
Outlaw	12	12	14
Defense spending			
Decrease	36	38	43
In-between	36	40	33
Increase	29	22	24

Source: 1994 National Election Study.

tion. This analysis yields results that are consistent with the notion that turnout mattered. Whereas 56 percent of respondents who said they voted preferred Republican House candidates, only 45 percent of registered nonvoters did so. Unregistered respondents were virtually identical to voters on this measure, with 54 percent rating the Republican candidate higher than the Democratic one.

A more complex and indirect method of estimating the impact of higher turnout is to apply the criteria we know that voters employed, as Craig Brians and I did with 1994 NES data.[8] We estimated a logistic regression equation predicting the 1994 House vote based on the key factors of party identification, ideology, issue judgments, and incumbency status. Then by substituting information about nonvoters into the equation, we estimated their candidate preferences, assuming that they would weight these factors similarly. Although this is purely an assumption, we believe it is quite reasonable in the aggregate.[9] We found that registered nonvoters would have favored Democratic candidates by about 9 percent more than actual voters.

It is important to note that these registrants are mostly experienced voters; almost two-thirds of them reported voting in the previous presidential election, thereby largely accounting for the difference between 1992's 55 percent (of the voting-age population) turnout as compared with the 39 percent turnout in 1994. What if all these citizens who turned out in 1992 had continued to vote in 1994? They would have cast 29 percent of the votes (16/55 = .29). Assuming a uniform mobilization across the United States, and that they would have supported the Republicans at a rate of about 9 percent less than actual voters, these extra voters could have reduced the GOP's national percentage of the two-party vote by 2.6 percent (9% × 29% = 2.6%). Subtracting this percentage from Republican vote percentages in each House district yields a minority of 209 seats for the GOP, as opposed to the majority of 230 that they actually won in 1994. Thus it appears unlikely that Newt Gingrich would have become Speaker of the House if all registered American voters had gone to the polls in 1994.

Conclusion

Who votes does make a difference—both in terms of what issues get on the agenda and, in some cases, in terms of who wins elections. Most previous research on the subject has been far too concentrated on presidential elections, where a relatively high turnout rate (by U.S. standards) and the rarity of a very close outcome reduces the odds of finding substantial turnout bias. The example of the 2000 presidential election, however, shows that who votes can sometimes affect even the outcome of America's only national contest. But the many elections in the United States provide a wide array of opportunities for the impact of turnout bias to be felt. Because most American elections have lower turnout rates than presidential contests, the possibility that who votes may determine the outcome is further increased. In general, the lower the turnout, the more reason there should be to expect that there may be a substantial turnout bias. It is not surprising, therefore, that turnout bias is rarely mentioned as an issue in the study of major national elections in Europe, where 70 percent or more of the citizenry typically participate.[10] In Australia, where compulsory election participation keeps turnout rates extremely high, scholars look at the question of turnout bias from a different perspective—asking the question of how much difference it would make if turnout were not kept so artificially high. The answer appears to be that Labor would receive about 5 percent less of the vote under a voluntary voting system.[11]

Many American elections are about as far away from the Australian participatory norm as known anywhere in the world.

When participation rates fall below 40 percent—as in every mid-term congressional election since 1970—there is good reason to expect that representation at the polls may be biased. To further extend the argument, one would expect that in primaries—when turnout typically falls below 30 percent—some important biases would usually be found. Indeed, it is generally recognized that the rise of presidential primaries has moved both parties away from the center as more ideological voters tend to participate.[12]

If there is to be a conventional wisdom in political science regarding the impact of turnout on American election outcomes, it should incorporate findings from a wide range of high-, medium-, and low-turnout contests. Future research should be directed toward further broadening the scope of elections for which we have evidence regarding the extent of turnout bias.

How Voting Is Like Taking an SAT Test

Another aspect of bias in the American electoral process that suddenly entered the American lexicon during the presidential recount battle in 2000 concerned incomplete ballots. Many Americans were shocked to learn that a small but significant percentage of voters had no presidential vote recorded—either because they made no choice or failed to make a proper mark (undervotes) or because they made more than one selection and invalidated their vote (overvotes). A fair amount of outrage also surfaced regarding the glaring evidence from Palm Beach and elsewhere that many people had no vote recorded because they could not cope with the complexities of properly marking a ballot. Voting should not be like taking a test, but it certainly appeared that many people who wanted to vote found that it was a test they couldn't pass.

Given the complex electoral structure in the United States, no one ought to have been surprised. Foreign observers have often noted that in their country people simply make a mark or two on a paper ballot, and wonder why Americans have created this complex (and apparently often faulty) machinery. The answer is that such machinery is necessary, given the sheer number of decisions American voters are asked to make when they go to the polls. For example, in 2000 Oregon voters were asked to choose among opposing candidates for seven partisan offices, up to four judges depending on where one lived, and whether to approve or reject twenty-six propositions. Oregon provides an extreme example, but every state asks voters to make more decisions than is typical in countries with parliamentary systems.

One way American voters deal with the many demands placed upon them is to skip items on the ballot. This noncompletion has generally been called "rolloff," or sometimes "voter fatigue." In a close contest, even a seemingly nominal percentage of voters who have no preference registered represents a potential swing vote, as the world found out during the Florida election controversy of 2000. Moreover, rolloff undermines the representativeness of an election and the legitimacy of the result. When many eligible voters stay away from the polls, the democratic ideal is compromised to some degree; this is even more the case when some voters do not have their views counted on questions before the polity. The fact that rolloff can even be studied in the United States provides a sad commentary on the excessive complexity of the American electoral process.

Voter rolloff is important not only in itself but also as an integral part of American participatory culture. This point can be demonstrated via an examination of rolloff's relationship to other widely accepted barometers of mass political participation. First, the level of rolloff in a congressional district is related to the turnout rate of the voting-age population. In 1992 there was a correlation of $-.24$ between turnout and rolloff, and in 1996 the correlation was $-.29$. These correlations are significant at the $p <$ .001 level, indicating that higher levels of rolloff were more likely to be found in districts with low turnout. Second, the degree of decline in voting from 1992 to 1994—known as dropoff—is also related to rolloff. The correlation between rolloff in 1992 and dropoff between 1992 and 1994 was .22 ($p < .001$).[1] This finding indicates that districts in which voters cast incomplete ballots in

1992 were also the most likely to experience the highest levels of turnout decline two years later. The fact that voters are more likely to roll off in areas where turnout is low and irregular supports the conclusion that it is a feature of American political behavior that deserves serious attention.

So common has rolloff become in California, for example, that the secretary of state's office now separately reports the number of voters who do not cast votes for particular races. The basic findings from California in 1994 are presented in Table 6.1 for all offices and propositions that were on the ballot throughout the state. Notably, they do not support the notion that some voters simply become fatigued by the length of the ballot at a given point, leaving the rest of it blank. There was a gradual increase in rolloff from lieutenant governor through the State Board of Equalization. The great majority of voters who did not vote for the Board of Equalization, however, then voted for the next item on the ballot—the contest for a U.S. Senate seat. Soon thereafter, roughly a third of all voters skipped items 12 through 14 on the ballot, which involved whether or not to retain individual state supreme court judges. The rolloff rate then fell to about a fifth when the ballot turned to a nonpartisan contest for superintendent of public schools and then to just under a tenth when the first proposition appeared on the ballot. By the time voters reached items 21 and 22, many had skipped a number of questions and fatigue could quite arguably have been setting in. Yet the rolloff rate for these two high-profile propositions concerning illegal immigration and the regulation of smoking was a mere 2 percent—the same as for U.S. Senate. More than one out of every eight voters then skipped the final two items on the ballot, but rolloff on these propositions concerning the courts was substantially less than rolloff in the middle of the ballot for the judges themselves.

The pattern of rolloff in Table 6.1 should be familiar to anyone

Table 6.1 Rolloff from gubernatorial vote by placement on the ballot:
California, 1994

	Ballot position	Rolloff percentage
Governor	1	0
Lieutenant governor	2	5
Secretary of state	3	5
Controller	4	5
Treasurer	5	6
Attorney general	6	5
Insurance commissioner	7	6
State Board of Equalization	8	11
U.S. senator	9	2
U.S. House of Representatives	10	4
State Assembly	11	8
Judge Kennard	12	35
Judge George	13	37
Judge Werdegar	14	36
Superintendent of public schools	15	20
Prop. 181—Passenger rail and clean air bond	16	8
Prop. 183—Recall elections for state officers	17	10
Prop. 184—Increased sentences for repeat offenders	18	6
Prop. 185—Gasoline sales tax	19	6
Prop. 186—Health services system	20	4
Prop. 187—Illegal aliens ineligible for public services	21	2
Prop. 188—Smoking regulations	22	2
Prop. 189—Bail exception for sexual assault	23	8
Prop. 190—Commission on judicial performance	24	14
Prop. 191—Abolish justice courts	25	17

Source: Office of the Secretary of State for California.

who has graded a multiple-choice exam in which the difficulty of
the questions varies back and forth. Voters are not suffering from
ballot fatigue when they roll off; rather, they selectively fill out
only the questions on the ballot that they know something
about. Just as students skip questions on the SAT that they do not

know the answer to rather than risk being penalized for a wrong answer, so American voters follow the same logic. Voters are typically exposed to much more information about a race for a U.S. Senate seat than for a seat on a state supreme court. When they see the former item on the ballot they usually have no trouble answering the question; when they see the latter, they often skip it, turning to other ballot items about which they have more information.

The contention of this chapter is that voting in the United States has become a lot like taking an SAT test, and that rolloff patterns can best be understood through such a framework. Such an interpretation is consistent with much of the existing literature on rolloff, but at the same time puts a fresh slant on the question.

Previous Research on Rolloff

Investigations into the causes of rolloff have produced a diverse number of studies and a wide range of explanations. These studies form a portrait of the rolloff voter as being less educated and less politically aware than voters who complete their ballots. The literature shows no consensus, however, on the meaning of rolloff as an act: the question of which voters are likely to roll off has been answered far more adequately than the question of why they choose to do so.

One set of studies has explored the physical aspects of the voting process as potential causes of rolloff, and suggests that it can be attributed to confusion and fatigue experienced by voters in the polling booth.[2] In this view, voters would ordinarily complete the ballot, but a number have been prevented or discouraged from doing so by some unmanageable or overly tiring aspect of the electoral process. Voter confusion and fatigue are said to be induced by extremely lengthy ballots, long and legalistic passages of text accompanying referenda, changes in ballot format, and new or complicated voting machines. These investigations assert that less-educated voters are more susceptible to any confusion that might be fostered by the voting process.

Others interpret the meaning of rolloff as a form of rational abstention, where the skipped item results from a voter's lack of information or interest.[3] The rolloff voter in this view passes over contests in which he or she sees no benefit to voting. Seen from this perspective, people pick and choose their way down the ballot, searching for items that they are familiar with and issues that capture their interest. They vote on those items and skip the rest. Such studies do not necessarily contradict findings that rolloff voters are less educated and less politically aware. The key point in this view, however, is not that voters who skip an item are uneducated, confused, or fatigued, but rather that they have insufficient information upon which to make a decision.

One of the problems in the rolloff literature is that some studies have looked at aggregate election returns whereas others have examined survey data. Furthermore, these studies have varied depending on the type of election and locality under examination. In this chapter, aggregate and survey data are both employed, as well as a unique source of actual ballot records. The first two sources of data examine the same dependent variable—rolloff from presidential to House voting. This focus offers the added advantage of being the only political office for which rolloff can be calculated across the nation at one point in time. The ballot data then allow an analysis of all the major electoral choices for a few selected areas.

A District-Level Analysis

The aggregate data employed here are derived from presidential and House election returns by congressional district in 1992 and

1996. Districts where a major party failed to nominate a candidate for the House have been excluded, because it makes little sense to analyze cases of abstention when there is no meaningful choice to be made. Overall, where contested races occurred, 6.0 percent of presidential voters skipped the House race in 1992 and 4.9 percent did so in 1996. These millions of partial voters are worth scrutiny.

In examining the variables related to rolloff by congressional district, my analysis is guided by the factors that are known to be associated with turnout in general. Rational choice theory, for example, holds that people are more likely to participate if an election is close, thereby increasing the benefits of voting. Extending this argument to rolloff involves considering the costs of voting as well. By skipping a contest that is not likely to be close, the information and time costs will be reduced for the voter. As can be seen in Table 6.2, rolloff percentages do indeed rise as the margin of victory increases. Nevertheless, even in the most marginal congressional districts, over 5 percent of voters skipped the House contest in 1992 and over 3 percent did so in 1996. The problem of voter rolloff is therefore due to more than just uncompetitive elections.

Another factor involving the costs of voting is institutional differences in ballot format. Jack Walker found that rolloff could be attributed to one physical aspect of the ballots themselves—the use of either party-column or office-bloc ballots.[4] In the former type, voters are presented with each party's candidates down a column and hence it is easier for someone to locate all the candidates of his or her party and simply vote on this basis alone. These days, however, even Indiana—the founder of the party-column ballot—has counties that vote with small punch cards that make it impossible to print all of a party's candidates down a single column.[5] What Indiana and some other states still have across all counties is the straight party ticket option, which en-

Table 6.2 Mean percentage rolloff in contested House districts by district characteristics (*N* of districts in parentheses)

	1992	1996
Winning House margin		
Under 10%	5.3	3.4
	(82)	(78)
Between 10% and 20%	4.9	3.4
	(82)	(69)
Between 20% and 30%	6.0	4.3
	(72)	(77)
Over 30%	6.9	6.3
	(164)	(180)
Straight party ticket option	5.1	3.3
	(144)	(141)
No straight party ticket option	6.6	5.7
	(256)	(263)
African-American population		
Under 10%	6.0	4.7
	(251)	(256)
Between 10% and 30%	5.9	4.5
	(76)	(75)
Over 30%	7.8	7.3
	(33)	(38)
College educated		
Under 35%	7.5	4.7
	(54)	(58)
Between 35% and 50%	5.8	4.8
	(196)	(202)
Over 50%	5.8	4.6
	(127)	(127)

Table 6.2 (continued)

	1992	1996
New York City metro area	17.2	16.4
	(14)	(18)
Northeast excluding New York City	8.1	5.9
	(66)	(70)
Midwest	4.7	3.1
	(101)	(101)
South	5.9	4.4
	(129)	(125)
West	4.6	4.3
	(90)	(91)
House minor-party candidate present	6.0	4.5
	(227)	(284)
No minor-party candidate for House	6.1	5.8
	(169)	(120)
1-district state	3.1	1.3
	(7)	(7)
2–4 districts in state	4.4	2.3
	(31)	(30)
5–9 districts in state	5.8	3.7
	(108)	(108)
10–19 districts in state	6.2	4.2
	(97)	(97)
Over 20 districts in state	6.6	6.7
	(157)	(162)
Nationwide	6.0	4.9
	(400)	(404)

Sources: Official election returns; *The 1998 Almanac of American Politics.*

ables voters to cast a vote for all of a party's candidates with a single punch or pull of the lever. Because this option minimizes the costs of voting for multiple offices, rolloff should be expected to be less in these states. Such a hypothesis is supported by the aggregate data presented in Table 6.2.

A sociological perspective on participation would lead to an expectation of higher levels of rolloff in areas with a high percentage of minorities and where the average level of socioeconomic status is low. Numerous studies have found that rolloff is greater among members of minority groups and those with low levels of education,[6] and of course this aspect drew national attention during the Florida election controversy in 2000. In both 1992 and 1996, districts where the population was over 30 percent African American had average rolloff figures of over 7 percent, which was substantially above the national average. It might be hypothesized that these districts had a high degree of rolloff because their voters tend to be among the least well educated in the nation. However, there is rather limited evidence for any relationship between education and rolloff in the congressional district data. In 1992 the districts with the lowest level of education had somewhat higher rolloff than other districts, but this was not the case in 1996. Furthermore, there was no difference in either year between districts with medium and high levels of education. An alternative explanation for the high rolloff rates in areas with high concentrations of African Americans may be that racial minorities do not perceive lower-level offices as being salient and are therefore less likely to seek out information about them. Past research has suggested that minorities may view lower-level offices as unresponsive to the needs of their community.[7] African-American voters are much more likely to participate in a lower-level contest when African-American candidates are involved.[8]

The most surprising district-level finding is the pattern of rolloff across regions. Given the historical pattern of low turnout in the South, rolloff should be highest below the Mason-Dixon line. Instead, the Northeast exhibits the most rolloff. When the analysis is narrowed to the state level, it is clear that New York has by far the highest rolloff level. This oddity is not consistent throughout the state, but rather is centered in the New York City metropolitan area. In the contested districts around the Big Apple, rolloff averaged an astonishing 17.2 percent in 1992 and 16.4 percent in 1996. Except for one case in 1996—where the wife of a victim of the Long Island train massacre won a race that attracted national media attention—each district had above-average rolloff levels. Perhaps the high level of population density in this area leads voters to be unaware and/or unconcerned with their House race. However, an examination of voting in statewide races in 1994 demonstrates that the phenomenon of high rolloff in New York City is evident in more than just House races.[9] I can only conclude that there is something unique about the culture of this city that makes its residents particularly prone to cast incomplete ballots.

The higher information costs that citizens of populous states like New York no doubt face in learning about their House race are nevertheless a factor in explaining variations in rolloff. This factor is particularly apparent when examining rolloff figures for districts that constitute a whole state, and hence where a House race resembles a Senate contest. In both 1992 and 1996, these seven districts had the lowest rolloff levels of any category examined in Table 6.2. Furthermore, in each year there is a linear relationship between the size of the state and rolloff. This relationship probably exists because voters who live in small states are more likely to know which district they live in, as well as to have the opportunity to learn about the candidates from their local media.

A final variable that influences the amount of information a voter may have about a House race is the sheer number of candi-

Table 6.3   Predicting the rolloff percentage in contested house districts in 1992 and 1996

	Regression estimates			
	1992		1996	
	Coefficient	Standard error	Coefficient	Standard error
Winning margin	.050***	.011	.045***	.011
Straight party ticket option	−1.300***	.378	−1.870***	.420
Minority-majority	.321	.590	.486	.661
Percentage college educated	−3.942*	1.784	.082	1.912
New York City	11.188***	.913	10.503***	.927
Northeast excluding NYC	2.868***	.458	2.049***	.489
Minor-party candidate in House race	−.122	.364	−1.072*	.420
State has under five congressional districts	−1.875***	.567	−2.295***	.641
Constant	6.306***	.921	4.125***	1.038
Multiple R	.65		.66	
N	376		386	

*$p < .05$.   **$p < .01$.   ***$p < .001$.

Sources: Official election returns; *The 1998 Almanac of American Politics.*

dates running for the seat. If a minor-party candidate is running, then this only adds to the available information. Perhaps more important, having a minor-party candidate on the ballot gives the voter who is dissatisfied with the Democratic and Republican nominees a further option other than abstaining. The evidence for this theory is mixed, however, with districts lacking a minor-party candidate having higher levels of rolloff in 1996 but not in 1992.

Taken together, the variables examined thus far point to an informational explanation for rolloff. Table 6.3 presents a regression equation for each year predicting the percentage of rolloff in contested congressional districts based on the variables reviewed above. Besides the unexplained regional variations, the three variables that are significant at the $p < .001$ level in both 1992 and 1996 are the margin of victory, the presence or absence of the straight party ticket option, and whether or not the state has fewer than five districts. Interestingly, whether a district has a minority majority has no impact on rolloff once other variables are controlled for, and the percentage of the district which is college educated is only barely significant in 1992. Thus the political circumstances of the election appear far more important than the demographic makeup of the district in explaining rolloff. This conclusion is further reinforced by the survey data, which enable a more precise analysis of who the rolloff voters are as well as the political information they possess.

Survey Data on Rolloff

District-level data and election returns have proved useful in establishing broad patterns. Survey data are required, however, in order to examine the various specific factors that influence whether individuals roll off or not. Although survey data allow more refined hypotheses, they also have some weaknesses that should be noted. First, because the percentage of people who vote for president but not for the House is relatively small, any one survey will have too few cases to analyze rolloff with much confidence. Therefore data from the National Election Studies of 1980, 1984, and 1988 are combined for this analysis.

A second problem is that of measurement error. Just as turnout is regularly overestimated in the NES, so is rolloff. Not surprisingly, people who misreport going to the polls have a rolloff rate over twice as high as validated voters. Although they have no trouble in saying how they supposedly voted for president, many are caught in a lie when asked about low-stimulus House races.

Hence cases in which respondents say they voted but that cannot be validated have been deleted.[10] Restricting the analysis to validated voters living in contested districts, I estimate that 9.3 percent rolled off in House elections during the 1980s. This still represents an overestimate, but one that is tolerable.[11] Another reason why the NES is bound to overestimate rolloff is that some voters will naturally forget about their choice for the House in the time between election day and their postelection interview. To attempt to control for this factor, the number of days between the election and the day respondents were interviewed is included as an independent variable.

Table 6.4 compares rolloff voters (those who voted for president and not for the House) and full voters on a number of characteristics. As expected, rolloff voters were interviewed on average somewhat later than full voters. In terms of the two best demographic predictors of turnout—age and education—it is noteworthy that the two groups are virtually indistinguishable from full voters, which probably explains why the rolloff voters went to the polls in the first place. Despite the findings of a number of previous studies that have shown African Americans to be more likely to roll off, only slight support for such a pattern is found in the national survey data.

The demographic variable that is most associated with congressional rolloff is marital status. Married people are more likely to become involved in community activities, and therefore would be more knowledgeable about the local House contest. Two other variables that are likely to promote awareness of local politics are also found to be associated with rolloff—stability of residence and living in a state with relatively few districts. It is especially reassuring that the pattern found in the aggregate data of lower rolloff in the least populous states can also be seen in the survey data, even though the number of NES respondents from these areas is necessarily small. There are even greater data limitations in analyzing NES respondents from New York City, but as with

Table 6.4   Rolloff voters compared with full voters in 1980s survey data

	Rolloff voters	Full voters
Mean N of days interviewed after the election	18.2	15.8
Mean age	46.4	47.1
% not college educated	49.6	48.0
% not married	44.4	34.4
% non-White	11.6	8.2
% who have lived in area under one year	12.4	6.7
% residing in a state with under five districts	4.3	8.2
% residing in New York City	4.7	1.7
% residing in a state without the straight-ticket option	71.8	68.0
% Independent	34.8	29.9
% who follow politics now and then or rarely	41.3	26.7
% who say they have no say in government	37.7	27.6
% who say politics is too complicated	71.3	65.5
% who say those who don't care about the outcome shouldn't vote	54.3	42.0
% not knowing which party controlled the House prior to the election	43.6	25.2
% recognizing neither House candidate	35.0	7.1
% with no contact with either House candidate	61.1	27.9

Source: Pooled data from the 1980, 1984, and 1988 National Election Studies.

the aggregate data Big Apple residents are found to have a level of rolloff far above the national average.[12]

Whereas the demographic variables largely confirm the findings from the aggregate data, the attitudinal variables and questions about the candidates allow an extension of the analysis in new directions. In terms of the psychological variables, those who roll off when it comes to the House race consistently demonstrate their status as peripheral voters. They are more likely to be Independents than full voters, less interested in politics, and less efficacious—all befitting their peripheral position in the electorate. And when asked whether those who don't care about an election shouldn't vote, rolloff voters are naturally more likely to agree with this sentiment than full voters.

It is when one turns to variables specifically dealing with the House of Representatives that the starkest differences are found between rolloff and full voters. One explanation for why rolloff voters are less motivated to vote for the House is that they are substantially less likely to know the most basic fact about it—that the Democrats were then the majority party. Even greater differences are found when one turns to specific knowledge about the candidates for the House. Over one-third of the rolloff voters were unable to recognize either major-party candidate in their district compared with just 7 percent among full voters. And three-fifths of the rolloff voters report having no exposure to either of the candidates—meaning that they had never received mail from them, seen them on television or heard them on the radio, or had any personal contact with them or their staff. The magnitude of these variables dealing with the House and candidates for it leads to an expectation that this may well be the most significant factor in explaining the rolloff phenomenon. In order to establish whether this is so, as well as the independent impact of the various factors discussed thus far, multivariate analysis is required.

Table 6.5 presents a logistic regression predicting rolloff voters from full voters employing the variables discussed above. Except for age, recognition of House candidates, and contact with them, all the variables are coded so as to expect a positive coefficient.[13] The direction of the coefficients are all in the expected direction, except for age, which is not even remotely close to being significant in any case. Importantly, none of the other demographic variables are significant in predicting rolloff either. Therefore, if minority groups, the poorly educated, and the unmarried are

Table 6.5   Logistic regression predicting rolloff voters from full voters

	Coefficient	Standard error
Number of days interviewed after the election	.005	.007
Age	.001	.005
Not college educated	.247	.177
Not married	.250	.161
Non-White	.073	.253
Mobile	.570*	.246
Number of districts in state of residence	.016**	.006
Resident of New York City	.540	.394
Resident of a state without the straight-ticket option	.136	.180
Strength of party identification	.230**	.082
Political interest	.161	.089
No say in government	.150	.087
Politics is too complicated	.079	.094
Those who don't care about the outcome shouldn't vote	.203**	.080
Didn't know which party controlled the House prior to the election	.398*	.174
Recognition of House candidates	.480***	.120
Contact with House candidates	−.686***	.114

$N = 2{,}330$.   % correctly predicted = 91.3.
$*p < .05$. $**p < .01$. $***p < .001$.
Source: Pooled data from the 1980, 1984, and 1988 National Election Studies.

more likely to roll off, it is because of other, more important factors.

The variables that were found to be consequential are all consistent with the informational hypothesis. The two significant demographic variables were mobility and the size of the state one lived in. As discussed earlier, people who are mobile are less likely to have sufficient information about the candidates, as are people who live in states where there are so many congressional districts that local newspapers and television stations do not have time to

cover them. Similarly, the reason that strength of party identification is significant in the equation is probably because people
with party loyalties can rely on the informational power of the
party labels on the ballot without knowing anything else about
the candidates. People with a sense of party identification are also
more likely to care about the outcome, and the multivariate analysis shows that respondents who felt that people who don't care
about the outcome shouldn't vote were more likely to be rolloff
voters. The major reasons why rolloff voters fail to cast a ballot
for the House, however, relate specifically to their lack of information about that particular race. By far the most statistically
significant variables in predicting rolloff were the number of
House candidates voters recognized and had some form of contact with.

Ballot Data

One of the weaknesses in using survey data to examine rolloff is
that the analyst can only look at a small portion of voters' decisions. Although it might be theoretically feasible in a survey of
one state or county to ask respondents how they voted on every
question listed on the ballot, it does not seem very practical. Respondents would probably find it difficult to recall how they
voted on many questions, not to mention tedious. Fortunately,
electronic records of entire ballots can be obtained from some
counties around the nation who are willing to cooperate with social science researchers.[14] These records provide both complete
and fully accurate accounts of individual voting behavior—there
is no measurement error at all. The disadvantage is that because
of the secrecy of the ballot one has no idea of the characteristics
of the individual voter. Nevertheless, the skip patterns for ballot
items are of interest, in and of themselves.

First, one can precisely ascertain the percentage of voters who skip at least one major decision on the ballot. In Los Angeles County in 1994, 48.4 percent of voters skipped at least one of the twenty-four offices and issues upon which all Californians were asked to vote; 19.2 percent skipped at least six of these items. Miami voters in 1998 had twenty-one offices and propositions that appeared on ballots statewide; 50.6 percent skipped at least one of these; 27.4 percent skipped at least half a dozen questions. In 1998 in Genesee County, Michigan (which is centered around Flint), 45.0 percent of voters skipped at least one of the eleven major decisions voters were called upon to make—six partisan offices, two justices of the state supreme court, and three state proposals; 23.7 percent skipped at least two of these eleven items. The data from these three quite different counties are thus remarkably consistent. About half of those who showed up at the polls skipped at least one major decision on the ballot, and roughly a quarter of voters skipped a fairly large percentage of the questions before the electorate. If this were a standardized test in school, many teachers would be pleased with these completion rates. However, democracy is not supposed to resemble a test.

An examination of individual skip patterns confirms that they look just like what one would expect from a test where the questions offer a fair range in terms of degree of difficulty. On a test, students who do well on the most difficult questions usually also have the least amount of trouble with the easier questions; similar patterns can be found in the ballot data. This point can be nicely supported by examining individual ballot patterns for the questions posed to California voters in 1994 and discussed earlier in this chapter. These questions can be divided into three levels of difficulty based on the overall rolloff levels displayed in Table 6.1. Questions were classified as "most difficult" if the state rolloff rate was at least 10 percent, "easy" if rolloff was 2 percent or less, and "medium-level difficulty" if the rolloff rate fell in between these two standards. Figure 6.1 shows that how well voters coped with

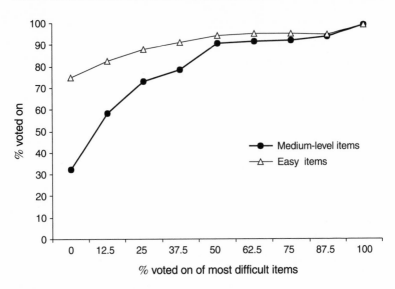

Figure 6.1 Completion rates for easy and medium-level ballot choices by rolloff on difficult choices, Los Angeles, 1994. (Data from random sample of 8,632 ballot images from Los Angeles County, 1994.)

the most difficult questions is predictive of the percentage of easy and medium-level items for which they recorded choices. As expected, the slope is considerably steeper for the medium-level difficulty questions, as even the least-informed voters were generally able to make decisions on high-profile matters, such as whom to support for governor and whether to deny public services to illegal aliens.

Although the anonymity of ballots makes it impossible to match them definitively with voter characteristics, it is possible to draw reasonable inferences regarding which voters are the most partisan on the basis of their choices at the top of the ticket. Surveys have consistently shown that those who split their tickets for major offices like governor and Congress have lower levels of strength of party identification. And being less attached to par-

Table 6.6   Average rolloff percentages for lower-level partisan offices by patterns of voting for top two offices

	Miami 1998 (governor and Senate)	Flint 1998[a] (governor and House)	Los Angeles 1994[b] (governor and Senate)
Split ticket for governor and Congress	16.3 (94,835)	3.4 (34,795)	8.9 (2,039)
Straight ticket for governor and Congress	6.2 (206,139)	1.1 (96,633)	5.0 (6,048)
Skipped one	47.2 (42,284)	25.1 (7,850)	45.4 (474)
Skipped both	76.1 (6,927)	80.1 (835)	54.0 (121)

Source: Author's analysis of actual ballot images.
a. Uses straight-party punch.
b. Rotates ballot position randomly.

ties, these ticket-splitters should theoretically have less political information to help guide them to make choices for lower-level partisan offices. Table 6.6 shows that this expected pattern can be found in the ballot data from each of the three counties examined here. In Miami, for example, ticket-splitters for governor and senator rolled off an average of 16.3 percent of the time on lower-level partisan offices (such as Florida's secretary of state and attorney general), compared with 6.2 percent among those who voted for the same party for the top two offices. Notably, in Flint the pattern is similar but the overall rolloff rate for the lower-level offices is far less. Two of the biggest reasons for this clear difference are the option of voting a straight ticket with one punch and the party-column format of the ballot. These simple procedures make the American-style lengthy ballots easier to navigate and apparently encourage higher completion rates. Unfortunately, the nationwide trend in recent decades has been to abolish such user-friendly aspects of ballot design in an attempt to make sure that people vote for individual candidates as opposed to the party ticket.

In all three counties, the rolloff rate reaches extremely high proportions for those who skipped both of the most important offices. These people probably had some sort of problem with the voting mechanism, such as the Miami voters in 2000 who failed to place their punch card in the holder correctly and ended up punching chads that didn't correspond to any candidate. But these mechanical difficulties are vastly outweighed by the informational problems that people face for offices that are not highly publicized. There is no reason to suspect that people have more trouble figuring out the voting system for lower-level offices; rather, many simply don't know whom to vote for, especially if they lack any cues to rely on such as partisanship.

Conclusion

This chapter has sought to show that even many of those who do vote approach the ballot like a standardized test, and as with any difficult test some people do not do too well. It is reasonable, I believe, to infer that if voting is difficult for some of those who manage to vote that others must be discouraged from casting a ballot due to the complexity of the task. To offer a classroom analogy, this is like inferring that the students who drop out of a course midway through the term are the ones who can't handle the workload and/or the complexity of the material. Of course, one doesn't know this for sure, as these students never take the test. But this logic will be readily familiar to anyone who has ever taught a class.

The 2000 election controversy focused a good deal of attention on the problem of properly recording people's preferences, but a larger aspect of the nonvoting voter issue is that many are overwhelmed with more questions on the ballot than they can answer. Those who worry about voters' being frustrated by ballots that are difficult to mark in the right manner should also be concerned with the sheer intimidation many Americans experience when confronted with a plethora of decisions to make on election day. When respondents who acknowledged not always voting were asked in a June 2000 Pew survey to agree or disagree with a series of statements regarding why they skipped elections, 64 percent agreed with the statement "I sometimes feel I don't know enough about the candidates to vote." By contrast, only 14 percent agreed with the statement "It's complicated to register to vote where I live." After decades of focusing on registration problems, it now seems time to get the question of ballot overload on the electoral reform agenda.

Yet the trend in recent years has been to put more and more offices and policy questions on the ballot. Serious thought ought to be given concerning whether so many offices really need to be decided by the voters. We don't vote on each member of the president's Cabinet or allow voters to choose a vice president of the opposite party of the president. But many states practice just this functional equivalent. Similarly, we don't put policy questions to nationwide referenda, because our constitutional structure provides for a republic governed through representatives. But many states and localities have procedures for bypassing elected representatives and putting policy questions directly before the voters, which policy entrepreneurs and interest groups are taking increasing advantage of.[15] Thus representative democracy at the state level has, on the one hand, been extended through a proliferation of offices and, on the other, been frequently bypassed through referenda. The result is what might be termed "hyperdemocracy."

The challenge of so much democracy may well have to yield to the harsh reality that many citizens will see such demanding ballots as SAT tests upon which they cannot possibly score well.

Scholars such as Ian Budge and Anthony Corrado have written with great optimism about the promise of direct democracy.[16] Yet as shown in this chapter, voters skip items on the ballot not because they are lacking in education or are members of minority groups, but rather because they do not have enough information upon which to cast a vote. If we increase the information costs, we can only expect voter rolloff to become a more serious problem than it is already.

In order for voters to cope with the demands of hyperdemocracy, they will have to obtain a good deal of political information through the mass media—a process with its own inherent problems, as will be discussed next.

Are Negative Ads to Blame?

The first real television campaign in 1960 offered much reason to be optimistic about how this new medium would promote electoral participation. The Kennedy-Nixon debates helped spur voter interest and bring a higher percentage of Americans to the polls than had been seen in quite some time. Political advertising on television was still in its infancy in 1960; these ads look almost amateurish by twenty-first century standards. The images were hardly striking, the messages represented simple themes of the campaign, and they rarely involved sharp negative attacks on the opposition.[1] All of this changed in 1964, as the Johnson campaign mounted a harshly negative series of attacks on Barry Goldwater employing the use of dramatic images that Goldwater jokingly said would have scared him out of voting for such a candidate had he not known him personally.

Few developments have altered the character of American election campaigns as dramatically as the rise of negative television advertising. Long gone are the days of the 1948 Truman-Dewey contest, when the two major candidates went through the entire campaign without once referring to their major opponent by name.[2] As the focus of presidential campaigns has shifted from the stump speech to the thirty-second ad, charges and countercharges have become both more frequent and more direct. Darrell West's content analysis of prominent ads in presidential campaigns finds that negative appeals have dominated the national airwaves since 1980.[3]

Not only are negative ads regularly decried as polluting our national political debate, but they are also accused of contributing to low voter turnout. Three days after the 1996 election, Bill Clinton and Bob Dole were asked what they thought were the reasons for the poor turnout. At his news conference, the president stated, "The more the negative ads are, the lower the turnout is."[4] That evening on "Late Night with David Letterman," Dole included "a lot of negative ads" as one of his explanations for the low participation rate. He then went on to remark that "people do get turned off with negative ads."[5]

If Clinton and Dole had been asked to back up their claims about negative ads, their aides would probably have quickly dug up references to the academic work of Stephen Ansolabehere, Shanto Iyengar, and their colleagues.[6] Through a set of innovative controlled experiments, they show that subjects who view a negative ad embedded in a news broadcast are significantly less likely to say they will vote. These findings are supplemented by an analysis of aggregate turnout and rolloff data from 1992 Senate races that appear to show that participation is lower in states where candidates employ negative ads.

Ansolabehere and Iyengar assert that "attack ads can be and are used strategically for demobilization."[7] They argue that political strategists intentionally employ negative ads to discourage segments of the electorate from voting and are well aware that lower turnout is the result. As Teixeira points out, however, it is easier to change an election outcome by switching the preferences of existing voters than by manipulating turnout.[8] Imagine an election in which polling shows that 100 million people are expected to vote—53 million for the Democrat, and 47 million for the Republican. In order to win by reducing turnout, the Republicans would have to launch negative ads that would cause over 6 million Democratic supporters to stay home. But if they could change the minds of just over 3 million Democratic supporters, then they would come out on top. Given that voting is a habitual activity, would it not be much easier to change the criteria on which 3 million people with relatively weak party loyalties make up their minds than to get 6 million to kick the voting habit?[9]

It seems far more reasonable to presume that the intent of most negative commercials is to convert votes by focusing on an issue that the sponsoring candidate has credibility in handling but on which the opponent is weak. As John Petrocik argues, each party has issues that it "owns," and a campaign is a contest to focus attention on those that favor it.[10] From this perspective, even the infamous "Revolving Door" and "Willie Horton" ads of 1988 can be seen as part of a Republican strategy to change voters' minds rather than to demobilize Dukakis supporters. Republicans chose to focus on law and order issues not merely because of the weakness they perceived in their opponent's record but also because their party had long cultivated an image of being tough on crime. Certainly the message got through to a good portion of the public in 1988. My own earlier research found that the most commonly stated issue-based reason for opposing Dukakis was that he had a "lenient policy toward criminals."[11] Interestingly, 74 percent of the people who made this remark in the 1988 National Election Study preelection interview later said they voted, as compared with 69 percent who did not make this comment.[12] Although there is no way of knowing whether these respondents saw the ads in question, the substantive message certainly permeated the electorate. The fact that respondents who showed an awareness of the ads' theme had higher turnout rates appears inconsistent with the demobilization hypothesis and thereby suggests the need for further empirical tests.

This chapter presents national survey data demonstrating that the demobilization theory cannot be confirmed on the basis of NES data from 1992 and 1996. In 1992 recollection of negative campaign ads was actually associated with higher turnout, and in 1996 there was no significant relationship in either direction. Furthermore, the aggregate data now available provide little evidence to support the notion that the advertising tone of Senate campaigns has an impact on voter participation.

Election Study Data on Negative Advertising and Turnout

In the 1992 National Election Study, an open-ended question asked people if they recalled seeing any presidential campaign advertisements on television and, if so, what they remembered about any of these ads. The NES changed the format of the second part in 1996, asking people who recalled seeing an ad to think about which one they recalled best, and then to say who sponsored it and what it said. Although the question format differs somewhat, in both cases one can identify which respondents remembered seeing negative ads, positive ads, or no ads at all, and then correlate this information with reported turnout. (Unfortunately, the NES did not ask a question in 2000 that would enable one to differentiate respondents who saw positive versus negative ads.)[13]

It should be noted that recall data does not measure overall exposure to various types of political advertising. In all probability, nearly everyone in the country was exposed to some advertising, both negative and positive, during the course of these campaigns. When Craig Brians and I conducted this research, we were specifically interested in which ads made such a lasting impression that people recalled them when asked an open-ended question about political advertising.[14]

Interestingly, when people were given the chance to say whatever popped into their minds about TV political ads in 1992, the most common response was a broad statement that there was too much negative campaigning. Responses that either Bush or Clinton had been engaging in negative campaigning were also quite frequent. All told, 18 percent of the respondents who were asked the initial question remarked that there were too many negative ads—either in general or by one of the two major-party candidates. These individuals who were disenchanted with mud-slinging on television should be the most likely to fit the profile of demobilized citizens if Ansolabehere and his colleagues are correct. However, the results indicate a mobilizing rather than a demobilizing effect for negative ads. The reported turnout rate for those who complained about excessive negative ads in 1992 was 6 percentage points above those who did not offer this criticism. In 1996 only 5 percent of the respondents complained about negative ads, but again there is no evidence for the notion that people who are turned off by them do not vote. The turnout rate for this group in 1996 was a mere 1 percent below the rest of the sample.

A broader cut at the data involves examining the turnout rate for respondents who made a comment about negative ads, either in general or about a particular ad. It is also possible to do the same for those who recall seeing positive ads. Ansolabehere and his colleagues argue that when people are exposed to positive advertising they become more likely to vote, whereas those who view negative ads are less likely to do so. However, the 1992 and 1996 survey data displayed in Table 7.1 do not support their experimental research. Recall of positive and negative ads are both associated with higher-than-average turnout. There was little difference between the turnout rates of those who recalled positive as compared to negative ads in 1992, whereas in 1996 those who remembered positive ads had the highest turnout rates. In both years, turnout rates differ little according to whether people re-

Table 7.1 Turnout percentages in 1992 and 1996 by comments about recall of positive and negative political ads for presidential candidates

	1992	1996
Did not mention negative or positive ads	72.2	69.7
	(562)	(577)
Said something about a negative ad	82.5	76.4
	(681)	(288)
Said something about a specific negative ad	84.1	77.4
	(321)	(230)
Said something about a positive ad	82.2	82.1
	(275)	(128)
Said something about a specific positive ad	82.0	81.6
	(245)	(120)

Source: 1992 and 1996 National Election Studies.

called specific spots or made general comments about the ads. Hence, in the rest of the analysis the categories are simplified to reflect whether respondents made any comments about negative or positive ads.

Table 7.2 compares the turnout rates of respondents who commented about negative ads, positive ads, and no ads, controlling for a variety of variables that are commonly known to be related to voter participation. Among groups that are most in need of political mobilization, recalling either negative or positive political ads is most clearly associated with higher turnout. An examination of respondents lacking a high school diploma provides an excellent example. Compared with people in this education group who didn't discuss a political ad, those who recalled a negative ad had turnout rates 22 percentage points higher in 1992 and 14 percentage points higher in 1996. Other groups that were especially likely to vote if they recalled either positive or negative political ads include young people, Independents, non-Whites,

Table 7.2 Percent reported turnout by recollection of ads in 1992 and 1996

	1992 Commented on:			1996 Commented on:		
	No ads	Negative ads	Positive ads	No ads	Negative ads	Positive ads
Years of education						
11 or fewer	39.3	61.7	50.0	47.4	61.4	70.8
High school graduate	69.1	79.2	79.5	66.4	71.9	73.8
College	90.0	90.0	89.0	83.5	81.7	92.9
Age						
18–29	59.5	71.0	78.3	48.5	59.5	65.2
30–49	74.5	84.1	79.9	70.1	78.2	78.7
50–69	79.2	89.0	93.5	78.7	81.6	90.7
Over 70	72.7	90.0	83.3	82.1	88.6	93.8
Race						
Non-Whites	54.7	80.0	71.8	59.4	79.2	88.2
Whites	75.6	82.9	84.1	72.1	76.4	80.6
Campaign interest						
Not much	43.3	47.2	52.6	49.6	49.3	50.0
Somewhat	74.3	76.6	76.7	71.1	76.1	78.8
Very much	90.6	93.4	90.7	95.4	93.9	96.6
Political efficacy						
Low	53.6	75.5	73.7	59.9	73.9	71.8
Medium	84.0	82.5	78.4	68.6	72.9	85.1
High	88.0	90.9	92.7	82.0	82.0	84.3
Strength of party ID						
Pure Independents	41.0	65.8	63.3	45.9	43.3	58.3
Independent leaners	68.7	85.3	84.0	64.0	77.9	72.2
Weak partisans	77.5	78.6	82.4	69.2	71.1	81.6
Strong partisans	85.3	91.7	88.0	86.4	90.6	93.1
Turnout in last presidential election						
Did not vote	34.1	52.1	45.9	20.7	31.1	34.6
Voted	93.1	95.5	94.7	89.2	90.4	93.5

Source: 1992 and 1996 National Election Studies.

and people who scored low on the efficacy scale. Groups that traditionally have high turnout rates, such as strong partisans, have little potential to be further mobilized, and thus recalling ads had only a small impact on their turnout rates.

In addition to the clear lack of evidence for the demobilization theory, the survey data provide evidence contradictory to the argument made by Ansolabehere and Iyengar that "negative messages tend to alienate nonpartisans from politics further and to discourage their participation in a tainted process."[15] Decades of survey research have demonstrated that nonpartisans are no less trusting of government than partisans, and that feelings of political cynicism have no significant independent impact on turnout.[16] Thus there is no reason to expect Independents to be demobilized by attack ads, and indeed the NES data strongly point in the opposite direction for 1992. The 1996 survey data show a substantially higher turnout rate for Independent leaners who recalled negative ads, but among pure Independents there is slightly lower turnout. Given the small sample of pure Independents who recalled negative ads in 1996 ($n = 27$), one should not make much of this anomaly.

Another key part of the argument made by Ansolabehere and his colleagues is that citizens' sense of political efficacy is reduced by seeing negative ads. This assertion also does not stand up when tested against the available survey data. Respondents' mean efficacy scores were significantly higher if they recalled negative ads in 1992 ($p = .02$), whereas in 1996 there was no significant relationship in either direction. If negative ads deal with issues that citizens are concerned about—a goal that every political consultant would no doubt strive for—citizens could reasonably infer from them that public officials care about what people like themselves think. They need not like the technique to recognize that politicians are at least trying to address voters' concerns.

By placing emphasis on issues that are usually different from those of the previous campaign, both positive and negative ads could well have an impact in bringing different segments of irregular voters to the polls from year to year. Core voters would likely vote in any event, and Table 7.2 shows that regardless of their recall of political ads virtually all those who said they had voted in the previous election came out to vote again. Among those who sat out the previous race, however, those who remembered seeing either a positive or a negative political ad were more likely to vote.[17] The effects of positive and negative ads on the turnout of peripheral voters appear particularly evident in 1992.

Finally, a multivariate analysis is required to rule out the possibility that other factors—such as following political news via newspapers or television—could explain the relationship between turnout and recall of political ads found here. Table 7.3 presents logistic regression equations predicting turnout in 1992 and 1996 employing a number of demographic, attitudinal, and media variables. On the one hand, it demonstrates that even controlling for all these various factors, respondents' recall of negative political advertising is significantly associated ($p < .01$) with turning out to vote for president in 1992. On the other hand, the coefficient for recall of a positive ad in 1992 was insignificant. In 1996 neither positive nor negative ads had a significant impact on turnout once a host of other factors are controlled for. Contrary to my expectations, the coefficient for negative ads is in the direction predicted by the demobilization hypothesis. However, the standard error for negative advertising in 1996 is nearly as large as its coefficient, which makes it lacking in statistical significance. Thus this analysis has revealed little evidence in support of Ansolabehere and his colleagues' theory about negative ads in the presidential election survey data, and one solid piece of evidence in the 1992 data pointing in the opposite direction.

In their 1999 response in the *American Political Science Review*

Table 7.3 Logistic regression predicting turnout by political advertising recall, media usage, and control variables

Variable	1992		1996	
	Coefficient	Standard error	Coefficient	Standard error
Negative ad comment	0.430**	0.161	−0.201	0.179
Positive ad comment	0.025	0.208	0.265	0.281
Newspaper political news index	0.035***	0.008	0.034**	0.011
Television news index	0.002	0.007	0.018*	0.009
Age in years	0.027***	0.005	0.030***	0.005
Campaign interest: Somewhat	0.656***	0.176	0.382*	0.167
Campaign interest: Very much	1.479***	0.223	2.046***	0.326
High school graduate	1.333***	0.197	0.843***	0.210
College	2.058***	0.215	1.621***	0.224
Gender (female)	0.441**	0.140	0.320*	0.153
Family income	0.051***	0.013	0.056***	0.014
Interview date: Days to election	0.012**	0.004	−0.005	0.004
Marital status (married)	0.208	0.149	0.672***	0.166
Independent leaners	0.503*	0.210	0.818**	0.265
Weak partisans	0.605**	0.206	0.728**	0.254
Strong partisans	1.284***	0.239	1.783***	0.294
Political efficacy (medium)	0.549***	0.156	0.237	0.176
Political Efficacy (high)	0.382*	0.182	0.452*	0.198
Race (white)	0.086	0.187	0.196	0.206
Constant	−4.934***	0.424	−4.422***	0.422
Number of cases	1,843		1,373	
Percentage correctly predicted	85%		81%	

*$p < .05$.   **$p < .01$.   ***$p < .001$.

Source: 1992 and 1996 National Election Studies.

Note: Entries are unstandardized logistic regression coefficients. The variables are defined in detail in Martin P. Wattenberg and Craig Leonard Brians, "Negative Campaign Advertising: Demobilizer or Mobilizer?" *American Political Science Review* 93 (1999): 891–899.

(APSR), Ansolabehere, Iyengar, and Adam Simon estimated a model using survey data that supported their claim of demobilization.[18] However, they used intention to vote as opposed to actual vote as the dependent variable. The two are naturally highly related, but there is a substantial difference between them, and it makes little sense in my view to use intention to vote when one has a postelection turnout variable in the dataset. Kenneth Goldstein and Paul Freedman find many of the assertions made by Ansolabehere and his colleagues to be erroneous on the basis of data from actual tracking of campaign ads placed in the top seventy-five media markets.[19] This new source of data provides comprehensive information on the tone, targeting, and volume of campaign advertising in most parts of the country, enabling Goldstein and Freedman to construct the best measure of ad exposure yet developed. Their findings for 1996, like those presented here for 1992, provide clear evidence for a stimulation effect of negative ads on turnout.

Advertising Tone and Aggregate Voter Participation Data for Senate Elections

To their credit, Ansolabehere and his colleagues do not limit their analysis of the demobilization theory to laboratory data. In an otherwise critical review of *Going Negative,* Larry Bartels writes that "the authors' thesis is considerably bolstered by the supporting evidence provided by this rather modest aggregate-level analysis."[20] This part of Ansolabehere et al.'s research involved assessing the advertising tone in thirty-four Senate races in 1992 and relating this information to aggregate patterns in voter participation. Ansolabehere and Iyengar summarize their findings as follows: "We estimate that if all of the Senate campaigns in 1992 had been positive 6.4 million more people would have gone to the polls. Rolloff would have also been cut substantially, leading

1.2 million people who voted for President to make their voices heard in the Senate as well."[21] Both the national survey findings reported above and other findings in this book lead one to question whether the advertising tone of Senate races could have anywhere near that much influence on turnout or rolloff. Regarding turnout, it is important to remember that voting for the Senate is only one of many decisions that American voters are called upon to make. It is unlikely that the advertising tone of one sub-presidential race out of many could have a measurable impact on turnout. As for rolloff, the previous chapter has shown that the primary reason voters skip a particular office on the ballot is that they have not had sufficient exposure to the candidates. As people learn about the candidates from both positive and negative ads, one would expect that rolloff would be reduced by more of each.

When Craig Brians and I set out to replicate the Ansolabehere et al. analysis and control for variables we thought they had missed, we discovered that their aggregate dataset was riddled with errors, only a small portion of which we detailed in our *APSR* article on the subject.[22] Our reanalysis of the data (after substituting actual election returns for their error-plagued dependent variables) revealed little support for their claims that turnout and rolloff were worse in states that saw negative advertising campaigns for the Senate in 1992.

In response, Ansolabehere, Iyengar, and Simon present a complex multivariate model that they claim supports the demobilization hypothesis.[23] But because so many factors influence a state's turnout level (see Chapter 1), it is difficult in this type of aggregate data analysis to take them all into account in focusing on just the states with Senate races in a given year. The Ansolabehere, Iyengar, and Simon model suffers from such problems. In particular, it includes 1988 turnout as an independent variable, which has a .95 correlation with the dependent variable of

1992 turnout. Thus at most the authors are predicting the marginal changes in turnout from 1988 to 1992—and doing so without taking into account the tone of Senate races in the former year.

It is thus valuable to now have measurements of advertising tone for Senate races from two points in time, thereby enabling a panel-style analysis that removes the need to take statewide characteristics into account. Coding equivalent to that of Ansolabehere et al.'s for 1992 can be derived from data collected in the Brennan Center's "Buying Time" study of television advertising in the 1998 congressional elections.[24] Just over half of the states had campaigns that had the same tone in each year, as would be expected given that many of the Senate candidates from 1992 were running for reelection in 1998. There were eight states, however, that experienced campaigns that were more positive in tone in the latter year, and five states had more negative races. Contrary to the expectations of the demobilization hypothesis, states that had more negative races experienced the least amount of turnout decline from 1992 to 1998. A much stronger predictor of turnout decline, though, is change in the margin of victory; this variable explains 28 percent of the variance in turnout change, as opposed to just 2 percent for the variable measuring change in advertising tone.

Change in the margin of victory is also highly correlated (.66) with change in advertising tone. It should not be surprising to find that as races become closer, political advertising becomes more negative. Candidates without resources to mount a competitive campaign rarely bother to initiate attacks, and infrequently engender them from the front-runner. The strength of this relationship makes it impossible to apply multivariate techniques to sort out the independent impact of changes in advertising tone on turnout.[25] But given that the negative ads increase as races get closer and that these races saw less turnout decline from 1992 to

1998, it is difficult to see how these ads could have discouraged people from voting.

As for rolloff, in a midterm year such as 1998 the only way to calculate this would be to calculate the difference in the number of votes cast for governor versus senator. (Fortunately, about two-thirds of these states did have both races in 1998.) The results show little variation that can be related to advertising tone, or any other factor. The mean rolloff rate from governor to senator was a mere 0.8 percent, and the standard deviation was just 1.3 percent. This finding indicates that voters are generally exposed to a roughly equivalent amount about candidates for these two offices, and rarely decide to abstain from voting on just one of them. Neither change in the margin of the Senate race nor advertising tone is significantly related to changes in rolloff.[26]

These survey and aggregate results, which fail to provide any support for the claim that negative ads discourage people from voting, are quite consistent with the vast majority of studies that have been done on the subject. In a comprehensive meta-analysis, which reviewed the findings of fifty-two studies that addressed the impact of negative political advertising, Richard Lau and his colleagues found that the empirical evidence is too mixed and the effects too small in magnitude to back up the demobilization hypothesis. They state: "Participatory democracy may be on the wane in the United States, but the evidence reviewed here suggests that negative political advertising has relatively little to do with it."[27] In profession as contentious as political science, where little is rarely settled definitively, it is impressive how quickly a near-consensus has arisen in favor of the conclusion that negative ads probably do not discourage people from voting.

Conclusion

At the end of the infamous "Daisy Girl" commercial—the precursor of today's negative ads—the announcer says, "Vote for President Johnson on November 3rd: the stakes are too high for you to stay home." It is my view that negative ads have usually been about raising issues that will win votes, and hence convince people that the stakes are indeed worthy of their participation. If negative commercials persuade people that the choice between the candidates is an important one, ads are more likely to increase rather than decrease turnout.

The fact that the vast majority of real-world studies do not provide support for Ansolabehere and his colleagues' demobilization hypothesis does not necessarily mean that their experimental results are flawed.[28] It is widely recognized that experimental research can sometimes have great internal validity but rather limited external validity. In this case, one can easily envision an experimental subject feeling contempt for politics immediately after being exposed to a negative ad and saying that he or she will not vote. When election day arrives, however, this same person will make a decision about voting by assessing whether the difference between the candidates is worth the trouble of participating. If voters gain important information from these ads, as even Ansolabehere and Iyengar demonstrate they do,[29] then they should actually be more likely to vote.

If one is looking for a media-related explanation for America's falling turnout rate, a much better candidate to shoulder the blame than the rise of negative advertising would be the steep decline in public consumption of newspapers. In 1960, U.S. daily newspaper circulation equaled 54 papers for every 100 members of the voting-age population; by 1996, this figure had fallen to 29.[30] Both the 1992 and the 1996 equations in Table 7.3 demonstrate that reading a newspaper often and reasonably closely is more strongly associated with voter participation than any of the other media variables. Thus whatever small role that television advertising may have played in mobilizing voters, such as found for negative ads in 1992, has been more than offset by the decline in newspaper readership. In particular, as shown in Chapter 4, recent generations have been less likely to read newspapers, which is probably to some extent why their turnout rates have been so low.

Politicians may find that blaming low turnout on negative ads is easy, but the blame is misplaced. A number of policymakers have argued that negative political ads are poisoning the political process and have called for their regulation. One bill that was introduced in the Senate to much fanfare proposed that targets of negative ads get free response time if the sponsoring candidate failed to make the charge in person on camera. Clearly, the intention of such a proposal is to discourage negative ads. Those who wish to do so ought to consider the beneficial aspects of negative advertising presented here. In the face of the cumulative scholarly evidence it becomes difficult to maintain that an awareness of negative advertisements demobilizes voters in the real world.

Rather than looking for ways to encourage a more positive advertising tone, policymakers ought to be focusing on ways to ensure that more people are exposed to the basic messages that the candidates wish to convey. In 1996 a group of prominent political and media figures came up with an idea to further this goal. They proposed scheduling a series of free prime-time television appearances for presidential candidates to address the issues. The Coalition for Free Air Time called upon the networks to turn over two to five minutes a night to the candidates in the month before the presidential election. In addition, the coalition suggested that these segments be "roadblocked"—shown simultaneously on all networks and interested cable stations so that people watching prime-time entertainment would be sure to see the candidates. The coalition hoped that this format would promote a nightly dialogue on the issues, with candidates making news with their replies to each other's previous segments. Most of the networks did eventually grant the candidates some free time in 1996, but the approach was a scattershot one. The segments varied from 1 to 2½ minutes, and each network chose a different time to broadcast them, which led to much smaller audiences than hoped for. The results from the 2000 election were similarly disheartening. These experiments over the last two presidential elections have demonstrated the necessity of adopting a common format and time for all networks. A law that would mandate such an approach is certainly within the power of the Congress to regulate interstate commerce.

But given the general wariness of big government solutions in American politics, the likelihood of such a bill's passage seems remote. As with most proposals that academic research leads us to expect would improve turnout rates, it seems difficult to even place them on the American political agenda, as will be discussed in the concluding chapter.

How to Improve U.S. Turnout Rates:
Lessons from Abroad

Americans need not be chastised for their low turnout rates, though any increase in voting participation would of course be desirable. Indeed, it is impressive how many Americans vote at present, considering the complex and non-user-friendly electoral process they are faced with. Political parties once played a much larger role in helping voters surmount the heavy demands upon them. As local party organizations and party identification have declined, both in the United States and throughout the other established democracies, turnout has fallen. The U.S. states that have seen the greatest turnout decline are those that once had strong traditional party organizations, which placed a high priority on getting out the vote and devoted substantial human resources to doing so. At the individual level, American turnout decline has been centered on the people who most need to have the electoral decision simplified for them through a strong party system—those with the least education, political interest, and life experience. The abysmal turnout rates of young Americans, who have never experienced anything other than candidate-centered politics, are particularly alarming as one looks toward the future.

Academics have often claimed that low turnout in the United

States does not produce any important political bias. But such a position is hard to maintain in light of evidence that young people are being ignored by political campaigns (who naturally assume that most of them won't vote) and that their opinions differ dramatically from those of politically powerful senior citizens on many policies. A close analysis of turnout bias in the 2000 presidential election and 1994 House contests also reveals that who votes does make a difference. Furthermore, as the world learned during the controversy over the Florida presidential vote in 2000, turnout bias in the United States involves not just who votes but also which voters get a choice recorded. Many voters apparently approach lengthy and complex American ballots as they do standardized tests, and all too often they fail to complete much of their ballot. If the complexity of the ballot foils many who manage to go to the polls, it seems logical to infer that a fair number of those who do not vote are discouraged by the sheer difficulty of the voting task.

The key to improving U.S. turnout rates, therefore, is to make the electoral process more user friendly. Given that other established democracies have more voter-friendly systems, there is much that can be learned from their experiences. As President Clinton was said to have occasionally remarked, solutions to most public policy problems have already been found somewhere—we just have to scan the horizon for them. This is certainly the case for increasing turnout. Gleaned from the track records of other countries, a number of possible changes stand out as particularly apt to get Americans to the polls. (As discussed in Chapter 2, there are no policies at the U.S. state level that have proved to be a clear success in increasing turnout levels.) They will be addressed in order of their likely effectiveness, which unfortunately is inversely related to the plausibility of their enactment in the United States.

Possible Measures to Improve U.S. Turnout

If in an ideal democracy everyone votes, a simple way to realize this goal is to require people to participate. This is how Australians reasoned when they instituted compulsory voting after their turnout rate fell to 58 percent in 1922. Amazingly, there was overwhelming political consensus for this measure; the Australian parliament adopted it following debates that lasted only 3 hours and 26 minutes in the Senate and a scant 52 minutes in the House of Representatives.[1] Since then, Australia has consistently had one of the highest turnout rates in the world, even though the maximum fine for nonvoting is only about $35 and judges readily accept any reasonable excuse. In his 1997 presidential address to the American Political Science Association, Arend Lijphart proposed mandatory election attendance as the most appropriate solution for inequalities in turnout rates.[2] He argued that besides increasing turnout, mandatory voting would also stimulate interest and participation in other political activities and decrease the role of money in politics.

In the United States, the first question regarding mandatory turnout would have to be whether it is constitutional. It seems inevitable that such a law would be challenged in the courts. A case of such magnitude would almost certainly reach the Supreme Court, and how the Court would rule is by no means certain. Yet there is good reason to believe that mandatory attendance at elections would pass constitutional muster. Opponents would no doubt object that such a law violates First Amendment rights. Still, a compulsory attendance law requires one not to actually vote, but rather merely to show up at the polls. An individual's right to abstain would thus not be infringed, because there would be no sanction against casting a blank ballot.

Another constitutional question would be whether or not Congress has the power to compel election attendance. Article I, Section IV, of the Constitution states that "the Times, Places and Manner of holding Elections for Senators and Representatives, shall be prescribed in each State by the Legislature thereof; but the Congress may at any time by Law make or alter such Regulations." This broad power to make regulations concerning the manner of holding elections could well be stretched by the necessary and proper clause to give Congress the right to compel attendance at elections. This extension would be similar to Congress's assertion of its right to draft people as essential in order to carry out its mandate to raise military forces.

The biggest obstacle to imposing compulsory election attendance, however, stems from the country's political culture. American political culture, based on John Locke's views of individual rights, differs from Jeremy Bentham's concept of the greatest good for the greatest number, which has shaped Australian culture. Regardless of the legal considerations, most Americans—including elected officials—would probably assert that they have an inviolable right *not* to show up at the polls. As the former U.S. attorney general Griffin Bell remarked during a brief discussion of compulsory voting at a 2001 hearing of the National Commission on Federal Election Reform, "that is not a free country when you are doing things like that."[3] With such a prevailing attitude, it is hard to imagine the proposal ever getting off the ground in the United States, even if other OECD countries start to adopt this procedure.

Beyond that, it is debatable whether we really want to force turnout rates in America up to Australian levels. People with limited political knowledge might deal with a compulsory situation by making dozens of decisions the same way they choose lottery numbers. In Australia, this is known as the "donkey vote," for people who approach voting like the game of "Pin the Tail on the

Donkey." Given Australia's relatively simple electoral process, this proportion of the voters is small; in America it would likely be greater.

Of course, just simplifying the electoral process itself would be another way to increase U.S. turnout. In 1930 Harold Gosnell wrote in *Why Europe Votes* that one of the reasons for America's low turnout is the fact that its voters are "given an impossible task to perform on election day."[4] Voters in most countries are faced with only one or two choices every time they go to the polls, whereas Americans typically are presented with dozens of decisions to make. Furthermore, they are called to go to the polls with mind-numbing frequency compared with Europeans, who typically vote once every other year. For example, when Vice President Dick Cheney was registered to vote in Dallas from 1996 through the summer of 2000, he was called to the polls for sixteen elections (only two of which he voted in).[5] Notably, Switzerland has also overwhelmed its citizens with voting opportunities, and it is probably not coincidental that they too have very low turnout rates along with major biases in participation by age and education. It is thus worrisome that the trend in recent years has been for many democracies to move toward the U.S.-Swiss model of democracy rather than the other way around. In Great Britain, for example, the Blair government has promised referenda on various issues and created more locally elected offices, such as a mayor for London (an election that not surprisingly drew a very poor turnout the first time it was held). In the face of growing worldwide acceptance of the principle that the cure for the problems of democracy is more democracy, it appears unlikely that America will soon reverse course, recognizing that there can indeed be too much democracy.

Yet another unlikely possibility is that America might join the worldwide democratizing trend by adopting a more proportional electoral system. As discussed in Chapter 1, evidence from around the world indicates that our turnout rates could also be increased if we adopted some form of proportional representation. In our winner-take-all system, many Americans rightly perceive that their vote is unlikely to affect election outcomes. Proportional representation changes this perception by awarding seats to smaller voting blocs. The threshold for representation varies by country, but typically any party that receives over 5 percent of the national vote earns seats in the legislature. With a number of viable parties to choose from rather than only two, people tend to feel that their party truly embodies their specific interests, and hence they are more likely to vote.

If Americans were to adopt proportional representation, new parties would probably be organized to directly represent the interests of groups such as African Americans, Latinos, and supporters of the new Christian Right. Although new parties would provide more incentives for people to vote, and particularly raise the low turnout rates of minority groups, there would be a substantial price to be paid. The current system brings diverse groups together under the umbrellas of two heterogeneous parties; a multiparty system would set America's social groups apart from one another. Proportional representation therefore hardly seems practical on the American scene and has never received serious consideration at the federal or state level.

What has received much attention is the goal of strengthening the American party system. Over fifty years ago, a committee of distinguished political scientists concluded that America's party system was functioning poorly in sustaining well-considered programs and mobilizing public support for them.[6] Numerous recommendations were compiled, all of which the scholars believed would facilitate a more responsible and more effective party system—one that would be accountable to the public and able to deal with the problems of modern government. The APSA report argued that among the many tangible benefits of a strengthened party system would be an increase in voter interest and participation.[7] In line with this theory, as the party systems of the major industrial powers have withered in recent years turnout rates have fallen, as shown in Chapter 1.

The American case presents particular problems when it comes to reinvigorating the parties, however, because unlike parliamentary democracies the governmental structure is not organized around partisan politics. Even as the American parties have become more ideologically distinct, as the authors of the 1950 APSA report desired, their political role has been diminished. The rise of television broadcasting dramatically altered how politicians presented themselves as well as how the public received political information. Many politicians have come to realize that they do not need the parties to get their message across, and voters who are no longer exposed to a partisan environment have became accustomed to focusing on the candidates.[8]

The current narrowcasting revolution, epitomized by developments in cable television and the Internet, is likely to have a major impact as well. The much-anticipated proliferation of television channels and Web sites will offer more information than ever before in a wide array of formats. Some observers see these developments as offering "the prospect of a revitalized democracy characterized by a more active and informed citizenry."[9] The problem with such a rosy scenario, however, is that it is questionable whether many citizens will take advantage of this new wealth of information. With countless available information sources for a variety of specific interests, it will be easy for those who are not much interested in party politics to avoid the subject altogether. The result could well be a growing inequality of political information, with a small group of committed partisans becoming more knowledgeable while the rest of the public slips further into apathy concerning the parties. This scenario is especially likely to affect the next generation of citizens entering the electorate, who will be the first to be socialized in the Internet age. The generation gap in electoral participation—already wider than it probably has ever been—may well become even greater in the near future.

Lest one despair of any means for improving turnout in America, a simple yet effective change could be made in election timing. As discussed in Chapter 1, countries that hold elections on leisure days have higher turnouts than would otherwise be expected. Learning from this lesson, the vast majority of new democracies have adopted this practice in recent years. It is doubtful that any American elections expert would recommend that a new democracy emulate the American example and vote instead on a Tuesday. So if Americans wouldn't recommend Tuesday elections to other countries, why should the United States continue this practice? By joining the modern world and voting on a leisure day, it is likely that American turnout would increase.

Many people assume that federal elections are held on Tuesdays because this was established in the U.S. Constitution. But this is not the case. Like many other aspects of the political process, the framers left it up to the Congress to establish procedures. During the first half of the nineteenth century, the timing of election day was shaped by the mores of American agrarian and religious life. Early November was seen as an ideal time of year for an election, as the fall harvest was over and in most places the weather was still mild enough to allow unimpeded travel over the primitive roads of the time. Holding an election on Sunday—the most common choice in Europe today—was out of the question at a time when Sundays were strictly reserved for rest. Furthermore, with nineteenth-century elections being occasions for drinking and gambling, Sunday would have been most inappropriate for a very religious country like the United States at that time. Because many people would not be able to travel to the county seat in a single day, Saturday and Monday were also ruled out, since choosing either one would make it difficult for these people to attend Sunday church services back home. Why Tuesday was chosen from the four remaining possible days remains unknown. But it seems clear that the law was written so as to rule out November 1st, because it is All Saints Day, a holy day of obligation for Catholics.

In the 1840s, a simple act of Congress established the first Tuesday after the first Monday in November as the date for presidential elections; this was extended to House elections in the 1870s, and then to Senate elections shortly after senators became directly elected. Americans have become quite accustomed to Tuesday elections, just as they have to other outdated practices such as the nonmetric system for weights and measures. State after state continues to set primary election dates on Tuesdays. In fact, forty-six out of the fifty states chose to hold their primaries on a Tuesday in 1998.[10] With such a well-accepted tradition, it will be difficult to change this custom. Furthermore, religious considerations still make weekend elections problematic. Although blue laws have largely been eliminated, there would probably be resistance from some Christians to holding elections on Sunday; Orthodox Jews would no doubt object to changing election day to Saturday.[11]

As an alternative to weekend elections, another possibility would be to declare election day a national holiday. This was suggested just prior to the 1998 elections, and though the idea did not seem to grab the attention of anyone in government then, after the 2000 election controversy some major political figures at least began to talk about it.[12] About a week after the 2000 election, the House Democratic leader Richard Gephardt stated that he favored some change in election timing, saying, "I think having this on a Tuesday is unacceptable."[13] President Clinton also offered his endorsement for changing election day. In his last official message to Congress he wrote that "we should declare election day a national holiday so that no one has to choose between their responsibilities at work and their responsibilities as a citizen. In other countries that do this, voter participation dwarfs ours, and the most fundamental act of democracy gets the attention it deserves."[14] The National Commission on Federal Election Reform then offered a bipartisan endorsement of an election-day holiday in its report presented to President Bush at a White House ceremony in 2001. Commission members noted that besides the added time to vote on a holiday, other advantages would be that more public buildings could be used for polling places and more people (especially students) would be available for service as poll workers.

One possible objection to this proposal would involve the financial costs of yet another federally imposed holiday. An ideal solution would be to move election day to the second Tuesday of November and also designate it as Veterans' Day, which has traditionally been celebrated on November 11th.[15] Combining the two days into one holiday would send a strong signal to everyone about the importance that the country attaches to voting. And what better way could there be to honor those who fought for democratic rights than for Americans to vote on what could become known as "Veterans' Democracy Day"? As former president Jimmy Carter said in 2001, "Veterans, including myself, would be very proud to have us choose a president and U.S. Senators and congressmen and other state officials on our holiday."[16] In offering bipartisan endorsement for this proposal, the members of the National Commission on Federal Election Reform stated: "We reflected on the notion of holding the supreme national exercise of our freedom on the day we honor those who preserved it. On reflection, we found something very fitting about that too."[17]

As with any proposed change in public policy, there will be skepticism about whether it will work. Electoral reforms have often been known to have unintended and undesirable consequences. Ruy Teixeria expresses doubts about an election-day holiday, noting that it is "possible that the gain in turnout from hard workers who could not vote may be canceled out by the loss in turnout from citizens who decide to engage in holiday activities not conducive to voting."[18] R. Doug Lewis of the Election Center is even more direct on this score, writing in the *Washington Post* that "most people would use the day to play golf, go shopping or do chores."[19]

Although no one can know for sure until an election-day holiday is tried in the United States, there are nevertheless good reasons to think that such criticisms are not warranted. If voting is indeed a habit, it is hard to imagine that many of the people who are already into the routine will skip voting just because they have more free time on election day. And the people who currently mention lack of time as a reason for not voting are disproportionately younger, and hence probably are truly busy on a typical workday; a holiday creates more time in their schedules to vote.

A recent electoral reform in Japan provides evidence that extra time to vote facilitates turnout, especially among young people. Following record low turnouts in Japan in 1995 and 1996, political leaders decided that something had to be done to try to improve turnout. Although Japanese elections have long been held on Sunday, there were complaints that closing the polls at 6 P.M. was too early for people who had plans during the day. Thus it was decided to keep the polls open for an extra two hours in order to promote more participation. Not only did turnout go up overall in the next two elections, but there is evidence that the extra time to vote made a contribution to this phenomenon. An *Asahi Shimbun* poll in 1998 found that when people were asked why turnout had increased, 27 percent mentioned the extended poll hours—a response that was especially prevalent among young voters.[20] And in 2000, the same newspaper conducted an analysis of voting turnout hour by hour, by age. They found that people in their twenties and thirties made up a mere 14 percent of the voters in the first hour of voting but 40 percent in the last hour (which would have been unavailable to them under the old law).[21]

Making election day a holiday in the United States is probably not the reform that would improve turnout rates the most, but it does seem to be the easiest to accomplish—requiring only an act of Congress. The change could be made on a trial basis, to see how it works. If making voting more user friendly by giving people more time to accomplish the task doesn't produce the desired results, Congress can always change the law back to the traditional date. At the very least, such a visible national experiment would send a clear message to those who don't vote that politicians do care about them, and that everyone's participation at the polls is needed for democracy to work well. As an editorial in the *New York Times* stated, the holiday might "add a sense of importance and specialness to the day on which we go to the polls."[22]

In a review of Australian voting procedures, Malcolm Mackerras and Ian McAllister observe that "politicians and electoral officials have gone to considerable lengths to make the system voter friendly."[23] Indeed, they proudly proclaim that "Australia probably is the most voter-friendly country in the world." One can only hope that observers of American politics may soon be able to write that the U.S. electoral process is at least moving in the direction of being more user friendly. Such a development could only help promote the goal of higher voter turnout.

Notes

Introduction

1. See Harold Gosnell, *Getting Out the Vote: An Experiment in the Stimulation of Voting* (Chicago: University of Chicago Press, 1927).
2. There is probably more electing going on now in the United States than in 1960, due to the rise of presidential primaries and the seemingly more frequent use of referenda. My argument, however, is not predicated on this necessarily being the case. Any increase in ballot length is not likely to matter all that much, because the saturation point has long been since been passed. Given the continuous presence of a long ballot (more than five items), what really matters for voting turnout is coping mechanisms for dealing with such a high level of demands on citizens.
3. Anthony King, *Running Scared: Why America's Politicians Campaign Too Much and Govern Too Little* (New York: Free Press, 1997), p. 2.
4. James M. McPherson, *For Cause and Comrades: Why Men Fought in the Civil War* (New York: Oxford, 1997), chap. 8.
5. See Angus Campbell, Philip E. Converse, Warren E. Miller, and Donald E. Stokes, *The American Voter* (New York: Wiley, 1960).
6. Philip E. Converse, "On the Possibility of Major Political Realignment in the South," in *Change in the Contemporary South,* ed. Allan P. Sindler (Durham, N.C.: Duke University Press, 1963).
7. Seymour Martin Lipset, *Political Man: The Social Bases of Politics* (Garden City, N.Y.: Doubleday, 1960).
8. Frances Fox Piven and Richard A. Cloward, *Why Americans Don't Vote* (New York: Pantheon, 1988).

9. Raymond E. Wolfinger and Steven J. Rosenstone, *Who Votes?* (New Haven: Yale University Press, 1980).

10. For the full time series on this question from 1952 to 2000, see George C. Edwards III, Martin P. Wattenberg, and Robert L. Lineberry, *Government in America*, 10th ed. (New York: Longman, 2002), p. 239.

11. Philip E. Converse, Angus Campbell, Warren E. Miller, and Donald E. Stokes, "Stability and Change in 1960: A Reinstating Election," *American Political Science Review* 55 (1961): 269–270.

12. Richard A. Brody, "The Puzzle of Political Participation in America," in *The New American Political System*, ed. Anthony King (Washington, D.C.: American Enterprise Institute, 1978), p. 291.

13. Brody reported the following equation for 1920 to 1960: expected turnout = 44.8% + 1.63% per election (R^2 = .72). I got the following equation for 1960 to 2000 data: expected turnout = 62.6% − 1.25% per election (R^2 = .76).

14. Consider some stunning examples of poor turnout in each type: (1) In New Ashford, Massachusetts, none of the town's 202 registered voters turned out to vote in the September primary election and statewide only 6 percent of the voting-age population participated; (2) in Comfort, Texas, an election for the local school board in 1998 motivated just 17 out of 720 registered voters to cast ballots; (3) in Texas in 1997 only 5 percent of the voting-age population participated in a special election. This occurred even though Governor George W. Bush stumped the state for a week, urging people to participate and promising that a "Yes" vote would result in a major tax cut. Ironically, one of the people who did not vote was Dick Cheney, then a registered voter in Dallas.

15. Samuel L. Popkin and Michael P. MacDonald, "Turnout's Not as Bad as You Think," *Washington Post*, November 5, 2000, p. B1.

16. In 1960 the percentage of noncitizens was approximately 1.4 percent; in 2000 the comparable figure was 6.6 percent.

17. For the United States, see Alexander Keyssar, *The Right to Vote: The Contested History of Democracy in the United States* (New York: Basic Books, 2000); for elsewhere, see André Blais, Louis Massicotte, and Antoine Yoshinaka, "Deciding Who Has the Right to Vote: A Comparative Analysis of Election Laws," *Electoral Studies* 20 (2001): 41–62.

18. See President William Jefferson Clinton, "The Unfinished Work of Building One America," Message to Congress, January 15, 2001; and the National Commission on Federal Election Reform, "To Assure Pride and Confidence in the Electoral Process," August 2001.

19. See Louis DeSipio, *Counting on the Latino Vote: Latinos as a New Electorate* (Charlottesville: University of Virginia Press, 1996), p. 131.

20. The Caltech/MIT Voting Project, "Residual Votes Attributable to Technology: An Assessment of the Reliability of Existing Voting Equipment," version 2, March 30, 2001, p. 7.

21. Campbell et al., *American Voter,* p. 95.

1. A Worldwide Turnout Problem

1. E. E. Schattschneider, *Party Government* (New York: Rinehart, 1942), p. 1.

2. William Nisbet Chambers, *Political Parties in a New Nation* (New York: Oxford University Press, 1963), p. 32.

3. Richard Hofstadter, *The Idea of a Party System* (Berkeley: University of California Press, 1972).

4. Richard McCormick, "Political Development and the Second Party System," in *The American Party Systems,* 2nd ed., ed. William Nisbet Chambers and Walter Dean Burnham (New York: Oxford University Press, 1975), pp. 95–96.

5. William Chambers, "Party Development and the American Mainstream," in *American Party Systems,* ed. Chambers and Burnham, p. 13.

6. Robert Dahl, *Who Governs?* (New Haven: Yale University Press, 1961) pp. 22–23.

7. Leon Epstein, "Political Parties in Western Democratic Systems," in *Political Parties: Contemporary Trends and Ideas,* ed. Roy Macridis (New York: Harper and Row, 1967), p. 127.

8. G. Bingham Powell, Jr., *Contemporary Democracies* (Cambridge: Harvard University Press, 1982).

9. Ibid., pp. 120–121.

10. See Russell J. Dalton and Martin P. Wattenberg, eds., *Parties without Partisans: Political Change in Advanced Industrial Democracies* (New York: Oxford University Press, 2000).

11. In order to make the data comparable to the United States, it is necessary to speak in terms of the voting-age population rather than in terms of registered voters, because many Americans of voting age are not registered to vote.

12. David Glass, Peverill Squire, and Raymond Wolfinger, "Voter Turnout: An International Comparison" *Public Opinion* 6 (December 1984): 52.

13. Roy Pierce, *Choosing the Chief: Presidential Elections in France and the United States* (Ann Arbor: University of Michigan Press, 1995), p. 104.

14. Ibid., p. 111.
15. It should be noted that Canada permits election-day registration at polling places throughout the country.
16. Jack Vowles, personal communication, 2000.
17. *Economist Newspaper*, "Decrepit," April 3, 1997.
18. See Helen Fielding, *Bridget Jones: The Edge of Reason* (New York: Penguin, 1999), pp. 165–167. And lest one think that such a tale of fiction would not be found in real life, I would note that a fairly prominent British political scientist mentioned to me off the record after the 1997 election that he himself had not been on the electoral rolls for the past several elections.
19. "Wooing Voters with Cash," BBC News Online, August 21, 2001.
20. Supporting this notion, Mark Franklin's model explaining turnout in twenty-nine countries finds that the voluntary registration variable is insignificant. See Mark Franklin, "Electoral Participation," in *Comparing Democracies: Elections and Voting in Global Perspective*, ed. Lawrence LeDuc, Richard G. Niemi, and Pippa Norris (Thousand Oaks, Calif.: Sage, 1996), p. 227.
21. See ibid. It should be noted that the second edition of this piece of work by Franklin contains a model that seeks to explain turnout variations over time for thirty-one countries. This model shows no significant effect for the election holiday variable. However, such changes in election day have occurred so rarely that it is hard to see how a model like this would pick up much of an effect. Furthermore, of the countries that did change their election date, many already had high turnout rates to begin with.
22. Jean Blondel, Richard Sinnott, and Palle Svensson, "Representation and Voter Participation," *European Journal of Political Research* 32 (1997): 250–251.
23. It might be asked whether conducting elections entirely by mail would not solve the turnout problem. Thus far, no OECD-member nation has experimented with an all-postal election. Britain recently substantially liberalized its postal voting regulations. Over 5 percent of the ballots cast in the 2001 UK election came in by post, more than twice the previous record. However, the overall rate of turnout fell dramatically.

In the United States, Oregon, Washington, and California have all made postal voting very easy, thereby leading at least a third of voters in each state to send in their ballots by mail in recent years. But turnout rates in these states have not shown any noticeable increase. In particular, research on electoral participation in Oregon—which as of 1998 moved to voting entirely by mail—has found that the desired increase in turnout has occurred only in low-salience elections. There was no significant impact on turnout in Oregon in either November 1998 or November 2000. See Michael W. Traugott, "Why Electoral Reform Has Failed: If You Build It, Will They Come?" paper prepared for the conference "Political Participation: Building a Research Agenda," Princeton University, October 12–14, 2000; and Jeffrey A. Karp and Susan A. Banducci, "Going Postal: How All-Mail Elections Influence Turnout," *Political Behavior* 22 (2000): 223–239.

I am not optimistic about the use of all-mail balloting nationwide, because I believe it is necessary to see the ritual of an entire nation going out to vote on one day to mobilize many people with marginal political interest.

24. See André Blais and Kenneth Carty, "Does Proportional Representation Foster Voter Turnout?" *European Journal of Political Research* 18 (1990): 167–81; Franklin, "Electoral Participation"; Andreas Ladner and Henry Milner, "Do Voters Turn Out More under Proportional than Majoritarian Systems? The Evidence from Swiss Communal Elections," *Electoral Studies* 18 (1999): 235–250; André Blais, *To Vote or Not to Vote: The Merits and Limits of Rational Choice Theory* (Pittsburgh: University of Pittsburgh Press, 2000).

25. G. Bingham Powell, Jr., *Elections as Instruments of Democracy: Majoritarian and Proportional Visions* (New Haven: Yale University Press, 2000), p. 29.

26. Walter Dean Burnham, *The Current Crisis in American Politics* (New York: Oxford University Press, 1982).

27. Frances Fox Piven and Richard A. Cloward, *Why Americans Still Don't Vote and Why Politicians Want It That Way* (Boston: Beacon Press, 2000).

28. See Jonathan Steinberg, *Why Switzerland?* 2nd ed. (New York: Cambridge University Press, 1996); and Kris W. Kobach, *The Referendum: Direct Democracy in Switzerland* (Aldershot, N.H.: Dartmouth Press, 1993).

29. Susan Scarrow, "Parties without Members? Party Organization in a Changing Electoral Environment," in *Parties without Partisans,* ed. Dalton and Wattenberg; Peter Mair and Ingrid van Biezen, "Party Membership in Twenty European Democracies, 1980–2000," *Party Politics* 7 (2001): 5–22.

30. Edward Banfield and James Q. Wilson, *City Politics* (Cambridge: Harvard University Press, 1962), p. 122.

31. Russell J. Dalton, Ian McAllister, and Martin P. Wattenberg, "The Consequences of Partisan Dealignment," in *Parties without Partisans,* ed. Dalton and Wattenberg.

32. Mark Franklin, Tom Mackie, Henry Valen, et al., *Electoral Change: Responses to Evolving Social and Attitudinal Structures in Western Societies* (New York: Cambridge University Press, 1992).
33. Powell, *Contemporary Democracies.*
34. Otto Kirchheimer, "The Transformation of the Western European Party Systems," in *Political Parties and Political Development,* ed. Joseph LaPalombara and Myron Weiner (Princeton: Princeton University Press, 1966).
35. Ronald Inglehart, *Modernization and Postmodernization* (Princeton: Princeton University Press, 1997), p. 43.
36. See David Swanson and Paolo Mancini, eds., *Politics, Media, and Modern Democracy* (Westport, Conn.: Praeger, 1996).
37. On the 1980s: David Butler and Austin Ranney, *Referendums around the World: The Growing Use of Democracy?* (Washington, D.C.: American Enterprise Institute, 1994).
38. Walter Dean Burnham, *Critical Elections and the Mainsprings of American Politics* (New York: Norton, 1970); Paul Allen Beck, "A Socialization Theory of Partisan Realignment," in Richard G. Niemi et al., *The Politics of Future Citizens* (San Francisco: Jossey-Bass, 1974).
39. Seymour Martin Lipset, *Political Man: The Social Bases of Politics* (Garden City, N.Y.: Doubleday, 1960), p. 187.
40. I consulted with Lipset on this question, and he agreed with this interpretation.
41. Lipset, *Political Man,* p. 206.
42. Philip E. Converse, "Change in the American Electorate," in *The Human Meaning of Social Change,* ed. Angus Campbell and Philip E. Converse (New York: Russell Sage, 1972), p. 324.
43. See Richard G. Niemi and Joel Barkan, "Age and Turnout in New Electorates and Peasant Societies," *American Political Science Review* 81 (1987): 583-588.
44. See Miki L. Caul and Mark M. Gray, "From Platform Declarations to Policy Outcomes: Changing Party Profiles and Partisan Influence over Policy," in *Parties without Partisans,* ed. Dalton and Wattenberg.
45. In any event, the trends for parliamentary and presidential elections in France are quite similar.
46. Russell J. Dalton, "The Decline of Party Identifications," in *Parties without Partisans,* ed. Dalton and Wattenberg.
47. Edward G. Carmines and James A. Stimson, *Issue Evolution: Race and the*

Transformation of American Politics (Princeton: Princeton University Press, 1989).

48. Arthur Miller et al., "A Majority Party in Disarray: Policy Polarization in the 1972 Election," *American Political Science Review* 70 (1976): 753–778.

49. See Martin P. Wattenberg, *The Decline of American Political Parties, 1952– 1996* (Cambridge: Harvard University Press, 1998).

50. See Swanson and Mancini, *Politics, Media, and Modern Democracy*.

51. Paul R. Abramson, John H. Aldrich, and David W. Rohde, *Change and Continuity in the 1996 Elections* (Washington, D.C.: Congressional Quarterly Press, 1998), p. 260.

2. Turnout in the American States

1. Raymond E. Wolfinger and Steven J. Rosenstone, *Who Votes?* (New Haven: Yale University Press, 1980).

2. Richard W. Boyd, "Decline of U.S. Voter Turnout: Structural Explanations," *American Politics Quarterly* 9 (1981): 133–159; and Richard W. Boyd, "Election Calendars and Voter Turnout," *American Politics Quarterly* 14 (1986): 89–104.

3. V. O. Key, *Southern Politics in State and Nation* (New York: Vintage, 1949).

4. This variable was constructed by adding the number of contested races between the two major parties for the U.S. Senate, governor, and president to the number of close races (as defined by a victory margin of 10 percent or less) for these same offices. Thus the index ranged from one to six in presidential elections, and from zero to six in 1998.

5. Committee for the Study of the American Electorate, "Final Report on 2000 Election," August 2001.

6. Robert D. Putnam, *Bowling Alone: The Collapse and Revival of American Community* (New York: Simon and Schuster, 2000), p. 19.

7. Steven J. Rosenstone and John Mark Hansen, *Mobilization, Participation, and Democracy in America* (New York: Macmillan, 1993), p. 161.

8. These data are available at www.bowlingalone.com.

9. Rosenstone and Hansen, *Mobilization*, p. 77.

10. Wolfinger and Rosenstone, *Who Votes?*, chap. 4.

11. Rosenstone and Hansen, *Mobilization*, pp. 208–209.

12. Wolfinger and Rosenstone, *Who Votes?*, pp. 72–73.

13. Actually, most precincts in North Dakota maintain a list of voters who have voted in previous elections. Someone who is not on the list may

vote simply by swearing an affidavit affirming his or her residency status. Because of the rural character of the state and the numerous, small precincts, workers at the polls usually recognize newcomers to the polls in any case. When Steven Stambough moved from UC Riverside to North Dakota State in 1998, he informed me that poll workers allowed him to vote because they had seen him around the neighborhood, though they did not know him personally. Since then, he reports that he is always known to the poll workers. For further information on the registration process in North Dakota, see http://www.state.nd.us/sec/novoterregistrationinND.htm.

14. Richard G. Smolka, *Election Day Registration: The Minnesota and Wisconsin Experience in 1976* (Washington, D.C.: American Enterprise Institute, 1977).

15. Some states were unaffected by the new law because they already had most of these provisions in effect or used election-day registration. Other states, such as California, offered legal challenges to the law and did not begin to implement it until ordered to do so by the courts. Vermont was unable to comply with the law at all because of a conflict with its state constitution.

16. This analysis excludes Oklahoma, which experienced a decrease in registration of 17 percent, no doubt because a long overdue purging of the rolls was carried out. Also excluded is North Dakota, which has no registration, and Wisconsin, which has no statewide registration system.

17. In 1992, 68.2 percent reported they were registered as compared with 65.9 percent in 1996. Similarly, although far more people were actually on the registration rolls in 1998 than in 1994, the Census surveys showed a slight decline in the percentage who said they were registered—from 62.5 percent in 1994 to 62.1 percent in 1998.

18. Rosenstone and Hansen, *Mobilization*, p. 208.

19. Joseph I. Lieberman, *In Praise of Public Life* (New York: Simon and Schuster, 2000), p. 159.

20. Robert S. Erikson, Gerald C. Wright, and John P. McIver, *Statehouse Democracy: Public Opinion and Policy in the American States* (New York: Cambridge University Press, 1993), p. 77.

21. Alexander Keyssar, *The Right to Vote: The Contested History of Democracy in the United States* (New York: Basic Books, 2000), p. 157.

22. David R. Mayhew, *Placing Parties in American Politics: Organization, Electoral Settings, and Government Activity in the Twentieth Century* (Princeton: Princeton University Press, 1986), p. 196.

23. Joseph P. Harris, *Registration of Voters in the United States* (Washington, D.C.: Brookings Institution, 1928), p. 6.

24. Smolka, *Election Day,* p. 7.

25. Craig Brians, currently a professor of political science at Virginia Tech, was a police officer prior to attending graduate school at UC Irvine. He pointed out during my Electoral Behavior seminar that he had personally arrested people for registration fraud.

26. This analysis was made much easier by the foresight of Wolfinger and Rosenstone to publish the information on closing dates for 1972. See *Who Votes?*, pp. 68–70. The number of days citizens had to register prior to the election in order to vote during the 1996–2000 period in each state were as follows: Alabama, 10; Alaska, 30; Arizona, 29; Arkansas, 30; California, 29; Colorado, 29; Connecticut, 14; Delaware, 20; Florida, 29; Georgia, 29; Hawaii, 30; Idaho, 0; Illinois, 28; Indiana, 29; Iowa, 10; Kansas, 15; Kentucky, 28; Louisiana, 24; Maine, 0; Maryland, 29; Massachusetts, 20; Michigan, 30; Minnesota, 0; Mississippi, 30; Missouri, 28; Montana, 30; Nebraska, 10; Nevada, 30; New Hampshire, 0; New Jersey, 29; New, Mexico 28; New York, 25; North Carolina, 25; North Dakota, 0; Ohio, 30; Oklahoma, 25; Oregon, 21; Pennsylvania, 30; Rhode Island, 30; South Carolina, 30; South Dakota, 15; Tennessee, 30; Texas, 30; Utah, 20; Vermont, 10; Virginia, 29; Washington, 15; West Virginia, 30; Wisconsin, 0; Wyoming, 0.

27. The 1972 to 1996 comparison finds that turnout declined by an average of 3.2 percent in states where registration had become easier, 2.6 percent in those where the laws were basically unchanged, and 5.7 percent in the states where registration became more difficult. The average declines for the 1972 to 2000 comparison were 0.5, 0.2, and 3.9 percent, respectively.

28. As might be expected, the Kennedy operatives were never too open about what went on in this respect in West Virginia. The best source is Humphrey's memoir. See Hubert H. Humphrey, *The Education of a Public Man: My Life and Politics* (Minneapolis: University of Minnesota Press, 1991), pp. 157–158. Also see Mayhew, *Placing Parties,* pp. 81–82.

29. Alan Ware, *The Breakdown of Democratic Party Organization, 1940–1980* (New York: Oxford, 1985), p. 203.

30. Ideally, one would want to have a measure of strength of party organization in each state in both the 1960s and 1990s. But this is available only for the 1960s, and it would be a considerable task to create a similar index for the more recent period. Given the near disappearance of such tradi-

tional party organization activities, it also might prove to be a rather fruit-less exercise, as all the states would now probably be ranked very low on the index according to Mayhew's criteria.

31. The means on this competitiveness variable are as follows: 1960 = 2.44; 1962 = 2.10; 1996 = 1.74; 1998 = 1.88; 2000 = 1.63. The decline is less for the midterm years because many states moved their gubernatorial election from the presidential to the midterm year during this period.

32. See Michael W. Traugott, "Why Electoral Reform Has Failed: If You Build It, Will They Come?" paper prepared for the conference "Political Participation: Building a Research Agenda," Princeton University, October 12–14, 2000; and Jeffrey A. Karp and Susan A. Banducci, "Going Postal: How All-Mail Elections Influence Turnout," *Political Behavior* 22 (2000): 223–239.

33. Robert M. Stein, "Early Voting," *Public Opinion Quarterly* 62 (1998): 57–69.

34. National Commission on Federal Election Reform, "To Assure Price and Confidence in the Electoral Process," August 2001, p. 43.

3. Types of Individuals Who Vote

1. Anthony Downs, *An Economic Theory of Democracy* (New York: Harper & Row, 1957).

2. Raymond E. Wolfinger and Steven J. Rosenstone, *Who Votes?* (New Haven: Yale University Press, 1980), p. 80.

3. William H. Riker and Peter Ordeshook, "A Theory of the Calculus of Voting." *American Political Science Review* 62 (1968): 25–42.

4. Donald P. Green and Ian Shapiro, *Pathologies of Rational Choice Theory: A Critique of Applications in Political Science* (New Haven: Yale University Press, 1994), p. 52.

5. As a result of the lack of variation either cross-sectionally or over time, the National Election Studies discontinued such questions after 1980.

6. Bernard Grofman, "Is Turnout the Paradox That Ate Rational Choice Theory?" in *Information, Participation, and Choice: An Economic Theory of Democracy in Perspective,* ed. Bernard Grofman (Ann Arbor: University of Michigan Press, 1993).

7. Angus Campbell, Philip E. Converse, Warren E. Miller, and Donald E. Stokes, *The American Voter* (New York: Wiley, 1960), p. 90.

8. Political efficacy is measured through an index of the following three agree/disagree statements which were asked in both the 1960 and the 1996 NES: (1) "public officials don't care much what people like me

think"; (2) "people like me don't have any say about what the government does"; (3) "sometimes politics and government seem so complicated that a person like me can't really understand what's going on." Inefficacious responses were subtracted from efficacious responses. This index was then collapsed so that −3 through −2 represented low, −1 through +1 medium, and +2 through +3 high.

9. In the 2000 NES survey the question wording was changed in an attempt to reduce the overreporting of citizen turnout. However, this worked no better than the old wording in this respect. Because of this change in question wording, though, I have chosen not to use the 2000 NES for purposes of comparisons over time.

10. Warren E. Miller, "The Cross-National Use of Party Identification as a Stimulus to Political Inquiry," in *Party Identification and Beyond*, ed. Ian Budge, Ivor Crew, and Dennis Farlie (London: Wiley, 1976), p. 22.

11. See Martin P. Wattenberg, *The Rise of Candidate-Centered Politics: Presidential Elections of the 1980s* (Cambridge: Harvard University Press, 1991).

12. Warren E. Miller and J. Merrill Shanks, *The New American Voter* (Cambridge: Harvard University Press, 1996), p. 39.

13. On the decline of efficacy and turnout, see Paul R. Abramson and John H. Aldrich, "The Decline of Electoral Participation in America." *American Political Science Review* 76 (1982): 502–521.

14. John Brehm, *The Phantom Respondents* (Ann Arbor: University of Michigan Press, 1993), p. 16.

15. Sidney Verba and Norman H. Nie, *Political Participation in America: Political Democracy and Social Equality* (New York: Harper & Row, 1972).

16. In 1998, Democrats with identifiable Hispanic surnames turned out at a 59.1% rate, compared with 54.4% among Republican Hispanics. The figures for those who were born in Latin America were 64.7 and 61.1 percent, respectively. The higher rate for those born in Latin America is due to their being older.

17. Peverill Squire, Raymond E. Wolfinger, and David P. Glass, "Residential Mobility and Voter Turnout," *American Political Science Review* 81 (1987): 45–65.

18. Ruy A. Teixeira, *The Disappearing American Voter* (Washington, D.C.: Brookings Institution, 1992), pp. 36–37.

19. Mark Gray, "Six Turnout Treatises: A Collection of New Explorations into How Americans Do and Do Not Vote" (Ph.D. dissertation, University of California, Irvine, 2002).

20. Wolfinger and Rosenstone, *Who Votes?*, p. 19.

21. Norman Nie, Jane Junn, and Kenneth Stehlik-Barry, *Education and Democratic Citizenship in America* (Chicago: University of Chicago Press, 1996), p. 17.
22. Ibid., p. 101.
23. André Blais, *To Vote or Not to Vote: The Merits and Limits of Rational Choice Theory* (Pittsburgh: University of Pittsburgh Press, 2000), p. 84.
24. Nie, Junn, and Stehlik-Barry, *Education and Democratic Citizenship*, p. 190.
25. Wolfinger and Rosenstone, *Who Votes?*, p. 59.
26. I also performed a similar analysis examining turnout decline by age and education from 1974 to 1998. The results were substantively similar. They are not presented here, but are available from the author on request.
27. Robert H. Frank and Philip J. Cook, *The Winner-Take-All-Society* (New York: Free Press, 1995).
28. Nie, Junn, and Stehlik-Barry, *Education and Democratic Citizenship*, p. 187.

4. The New Generation Gap

1. June Preston, "Chinese Observers Slam U.S. Voter Turnout," Associated Press, August 12, 1998.
2. International Institute for Democracy and Electoral Assistance, *Youth Voter Participation: Involving Today's Young in Tomorrow's Democracy* (Stockholm: International IDEA, 1999).
3. On Canada: André Blais, Elisabeth Gidengil, Neil Nevitte, and Richard Nadeau, "The Evolving Nature of Non-Voting: Evidence From Canada," paper prepared for delivery at the annual meeting of the American Political Science Association, 2001; on Japan: Karen Cox and John Creighton Campbell, "Generational Change or Periodic Fluctuation? Age and Political Attitudes in the US and Japan," paper prepared for delivery at the annual meeting of the American Political Science Association, 2001.
4. Benjamin Highton and Raymond E. Wolfinger, "The First Seven Years of the Political Life Cycle," *American Journal of Political Science* 45 (2001): 202–209.
5. Donald P. Green and Ron Shachar, "Habit Formation and Political Behaviour: Evidence of Consuetude in Voter Behavior," *British Journal of Political Science* 30 (2000): 562.
6. "The Soul of a Senator," *Time*, August 10, 1998.
7. Thomas Ferraro, "Gore Tells Young Adults to Get Involved," Reuters News Service, September 26, 2000.

8. The full time series results on this question can be found in George C. Edwards III, Martin P. Wattenberg, and Robert L. Lineberry, *Government in America*, 10th ed. (New York: Longman, 2002), p. 3.

9. Samuel Kernell, *Going Public: New Strategies of Presidential Leadership*, 3rd ed. (Washington, D.C.: Congressional Quarterly Press, 1997), p. 132.

10. Ruy A. Teixeira, *The Disappearing American Voter* (Washington, D.C.: Brookings Institution, 1992).

11. Because the level of difficulty of the questions differed somewhat, one should only examine the differences within a year and not necessarily infer that political knowledge as a whole has gone down.

12. Stephen Earl Bennett and Eric W. Rademacher, "The Age of Indifference Revisited: Patterns of Political Interest, Media Exposure, and Knowledge among Generation X," in *After the Boom: The Politics of Generation X*, ed. Stephen C. Craig and Stephen Earl Bennett (Lanham, Md.: Rowman and Littlefield, 1997), p. 39.

13. Michael X. Delli Carpini and Scott Keeter, *What Americans Know about Politics and Why It Matters* (New Haven: Yale University Press, 1996), chap. 6.

14. Raymond E. Wolfinger and Steven J. Rosenstone, *Who Votes?* (New Haven: Yale University Press, 1980), p. 38.

15. According to the 2000 Census Bureau study, 55 percent of people under the age of thirty were registered to vote compared with 88 percent among people sixty-five and older.

16. See "Don't Ask, Don't Vote: Young Adults in the Primary Season," report of the Neglection 2000 Project, Spring 2000; and "They Pretend to Talk to Us and We Pretend to Vote," report of Neglection 2000 Project, December 2000. These reports can be found at www.neglection2000.org.

17. "They Pretend to Talk to Us," Neglection 2000, p. 18.

18. Thomas E. Patterson and Robert D. McClure, *The Unseeing Eye: The Myth of Television Power in National Politics*. (New York: G. P. Putnam's Sons, 1976); and Craig Leonard Brians and Martin P. Wattenberg, "Campaign Issue Knowledge and Salience: Comparing Reception from TV Commercials, TV News, and Newspapers," *American Journal of Political Science* 40 (1996): 172–193.

19. Ronald Inglehart, *Modernization and Postmodernization* (Princeton: Princeton University Press, 1997), p. 43.

20. President Jimmy Carter, National Commission on Federal Election Reform, Public Hearing 1, Panel IV, transcript, p. 13.

5. Who Votes Does Make a Difference

1. Raymond E. Wolfinger and Steven J. Rosenstone, *Who Votes?* (New Haven: Yale University Press, 1980), p. 111.
2. Ruy A. Teixeira, *The Disappearing American Voter* (Washington, D.C.: Brookings Institution, 1992), p. 95.
3. Sidney Verba, Kay Lehman Schlozman, and Henry E. Brady, *Voice and Equality: Civic Voluntarism in American Politics* (Cambridge: Harvard University Press, 1995), p. 205.
4. This is based on the exit poll, which reveals the following pattern by age: 18–29 = 55% Gore, 40% Bush; 30–44 = 47% Gore, 50% Bush; 45–59 = 49%–49% tie; 60+ = 47% Gore, 51% Bush. The Census survey revealed citizen turnout rates of 33, 56, 62, and 69 percent for these age categories, respectively. The actual percentages of the Florida population in each of these categories were 19, 30, 22, and 28, respectively.
5. For a review of many of their findings, see Martin Merzer and the Staff of the *Miami Herald, The Miami Herald Report: Democracy Held Hostage* (New York: St. Martin's, 2001).
6. Angus Campbell, "Surge and Decline: A Study of Electoral Change," *Public Opinion Quarterly* 24 (1960): 397–418.
7. Samuel Kernell, "Presidential Popularity and Negative Voting: An Alternative Explanation of the Midterm Congressional Decline of the President's Party," *American Political Science Review* 71 (1977): 44–66.
8. See Martin P. Wattenberg and Craig Leonard Brians, "Partisan Bias in Midterm Presidential Elections," *Legislative Studies Quarterly* (forthcoming).
9. If nonvoters were to weight factors in the decision-making process differently, it would probably be because of their lower levels of political involvement and knowledge. Therefore, one might expect nonvoters to place less emphasis on policies and more on party identification. Partisanship already greatly overshadows the policy index in the model for voters, however, so it is doubtful that nonvoters could rely much more heavily upon it.
10. An exception would be the 1999 election for the European Parliament within the United Kingdom. It is considered a second-order election, which typically draws lower turnout rates than national elections throughout Europe, and the British saw record levels of apathy in 1999. Even though the Labour government was far more popular in the polls than the opposition Conservatives, Labour suffered a clear defeat when only 25 percent of the voters went to the polls. It would be hard to ex-

plain this result any other way than that the Conservative supporters were much more likely to vote.

11. Malcolm Mackerras and Ian McAllister, "Compulsory Voting, Party Stability, and Electoral Advantage in Australia." *Electoral Studies* 18 (1999): 217–233.

12. See Austin Ranney, *Curing the Mischiefs of Faction: Party Reform in America* (Berkeley: University of California Press, 1975); and Martin P. Wattenberg, *The Rise of Candidate-Centered Politics* (Cambridge: Harvard University Press, 1991).

6. How Voting Is Like Taking an SAT Text

1. This correlation is based on data from 367 districts that were contested by both major parties in both 1992 and 1994.

2. See Jack Walker, "Ballot Forms and Voter Fatigue: An Analysis of the Office Block and Party Column Ballots," *Midwest Journal of Political Science* 10 (1966): 448–464; Robert Darcy and Anne Schneider, "Confusing Ballots, Roll-off, and the Black Vote," *Western Political Quarterly* 42 (1989): 347–364; Stephen M. Nichols and Gregory A. Strizek, "Electronic Voting Machines and Ballot Roll-Off," *American Politics Quarterly* 23 (1995): 300–318.

3. See Walter Dean Burnham, "The Changing Shape of the American Political Universe," *American Political Science Review* 59 (1965): 7–28; John E. Mueller, "Voting on the Propositions: Ballot Patterns and Historical Trends in California," *American Political Science Review* 63 (1969): 1197–1212; Shaun Bowler, Todd Donovan, and Trudi Happ, "Ballot Propositions and Information Costs: Direct Democracy and the Fatigued Voter," *Western Political Quarterly* 45 (1992): 559–568.

4. Walker, "Ballot Forms."

5. George C. Roberts, "The Vanishing Indiana Ballot," *Proceedings of the Indiana Academy of Social Sciences* 26 (1991): 138–144.

6. Jerome Clubb and Michael Traugott, "National Patterns of Referenda Voting: The 1968 Election," in *People and Politics in Urban Society*, ed. Harlan Hahn (Beverley Hills, Calif.: Sage, 1972); James M. Vanderleeuw and Richard L. Engstrom, "Race, Referendums, and Rolloff," *Journal of Politics* 49 (1987): 1081–1092; Darcy and Schneider, "Confusing Ballots."

7. Charles S. Bullock and R. E. Dunn, "Election Roll-Off: A Test of Three Explanations," *Urban Affairs Review* 32 (1996): 71–86.

8. See James M. Vanderleeuw and Glenn H. Utter, "Voter Roll-off and the Electoral Context: A Test of Two Theses." *Social Science Quarterly* 74 (1993): 664–673; Richard L. Engstrom and Victoria M. Caridas, "Voting for Judges: Race and Rolloff in Judicial Elections," in *Political Participation and American Democracy,* ed. William Crotty (New York: Greenwood Press, 1991).

9. The New York City metropolitan area is defined as congressional districts 1 through 18. In 1994, the following rolloff patterns occurred in New York City and the rest of the state:

	New York City	Rest of New York State
Comptroller	16.1	11.5
Attorney general	18.6	10.0
U.S. Senate	16.9	7.3

New York uses lever machines throughout the state, so voting mechanisms are not the answer.

10. Because the NES has not conducted a voter validation study since 1988, more recent survey data cannot be used.

11. I have not gone through the arduous task of calculating the actual rolloff in contested districts in 1980, 1984, and 1988. Census data on rolloff for all districts from 1980 to 1996, however, show little variation over time. Thus it is reasonable to assume that rolloff in contested districts in the 1980s would probably be close to the range found for the 1990s.

12. The number of cases from New York City in the 1980s was just fifty. The rolloff percentage was 22 percent, which is quite similar to the 16 to 17 percent calculated from the election returns from 1992 and 1996.

13. Further details about the variable coding can be found in the appendix to Martin P. Wattenberg, Ian McAllister, and Anthony Salvanto, "How Voting Is Like Taking an SAT Test: An Analysis of American Voter Rolloff," *American Politics Quarterly* 28 (2000): 234–250.

14. I am indebted to Anthony Salvanto for tracking down this information and decoding it.

15. On policy entrepreneurs, see Daniel A. Smith, *Tax Crusaders and the Politics of Direct Democracy* (New York: Routledge, 1998).

16. Ian Budge, *The New Challenge of Direct Democracy* (Cambridge, Mass.: Blackwell, 1996); Anthony Corrado, "Elections in Cyberspace: Prospects

and Problems," in *Elections in Cyberspace: Toward a New Era in American Politics*, ed. Anthony Corrado and Charles M. Firestone (Washington, D.C.: Aspen Institute, 1996).

7. Are Negative Ads to Blame?

1. Kathleen Hall Jamieson, *Packaging the Presidency* (New York: Oxford University Press, 1984), chap. 4.
2. David G. McCullough, *Truman* (New York: Simon and Schuster, 1992), p. 670.
3. Darrell M. West, *Air Wars: Television Advertising in Election Campaigns, 1952–1996*, 2nd ed. (Washington, D.C.: Congressional Quarterly Press, 1997), p. 59.
4. President William Jefferson Clinton, press conference, November 8, 1996.
5. Robert Dole, appearance on "Late Night with David Letterman," November 8, 1996.
6. Stephen Ansolabehere, Shanto Iyengar, Adam Simon, and Nicholas Valentino, "Does Attack Advertising Demobilize the Electorate?" *American Political Science Review* 88 (1994): 829–838; Stephen Ansolabehere and Shanto Iyengar, *Going Negative: How Political Advertisements Shrink and Polarize the Electorate* (New York: Free Press, 1995).
7. Ansolabehere and Iyengar, *Going Negative*, p. 9.
8. Ruy A. Teixeira, *The Disappearing American Voter* (Washington, D.C.: Brookings Institution, 1992), p. 87.
9. Donald P. Green and Ron Shachar, "Habit Formation and Political Behaviour: Evidence of Consuetude in Voter Behavior," *British Journal of Political Science* 30 (2000): 561–573.
10. John Petrocik, "Issue Ownership in Presidential Elections, with a 1980 Case Study," *American Journal of Political Science* 40 (1996): 825–850.
11. Martin P. Wattenberg, *The Rise of Candidate-Centered Politics* (Cambridge: Harvard University Press, 1991), p. 121.
12. Nine percent of the entire sample spontaneously discussed this issue when asked what they disliked about Dukakis. Independents offering this comment were about eight percentage points more likely to vote compared with those who did not mention this issue.
13. The only question about political advertising asked in the 2000 NES concerned whether or not respondents simply recalled seeing political ads. Seventy-seven percent said they did recall seeing ads; these respondents

were 17 percent more likely to vote than those who did not recall seeing any ads.

14. See Martin P. Wattenberg and Craig Leonard Brians, "Negative Campaign Advertising: Demobilizer or Mobilizer?" *American Political Science Review* 93 (1999): 891–899. I am greatly indebted to Craig Brians for his collaboration with me on this part of the analysis. Details on question wording and coding may be found in the appendix to Wattenberg and Brians, "Negative Campaign Advertising." This appendix also contains an analysis of the factors related to negative advertising recall, including data demonstrating that this variable is not merely a surrogate for attentiveness to politics.

15. Ansolabehere and Iyengar, *Going Negative,* p. 112.

16. Martin P. Wattenberg, *The Decline of American Political Parties, 1952–1996* (Cambridge: Harvard University Press, 1998), pp. 55–57; Teixeira, *The Disappearing American Voter,* p. 33.

17. Respondents under the age of twenty-two were of course excluded from this analysis.

18. Stephen Ansolabehere, Shanto Iyengar, and Adam Simon, "Replicating Experiments Using Aggregate and Survey Data: The Case of Negative Advertising and Turnout," *American Political Science Review* 93 (1999): 901–909.

19. Kenneth Goldstein and Paul Freedman, "Campaign Advertising and Voter Turnout: New Evidence for a Stimulation Effect," *Journal of Politics* (forthcoming).

20. Larry Bartels, book review of "Going Negative," *Public Opinion Quarterly* 60 (1996): 458.

21. Ansolabehere and Iyengar, *Going Negative,* p. 109.

22. See Wattenberg and Brians, "Negative Campaign Advertising."

23. Ansolabehere, Iyengar and Simon, "Replicating Experiments."

24. These data can be found on the Web at: http://www.buyingtime.org/. All the same states for which campaign tone was coded in 1992 were covered by this study with the exception of five small states: Alaska, Hawaii, North Dakota, South Dakota, and Vermont. I considered contrast ads to be negative, as Ansolabehere and his colleagues did not distinguish between contrast and negative ads. In order for a candidate's advertising campaign to be classified as negative, at least 10 percent of the ads run had to be either negative or contrast.

25. I did experiment with multivariate analysis just out of curiosity. When

put into a multiple regression equation predicting turnout change, margin of victory change was significant at $p < .0001$, and the direction of the sign for advertising tone reversed from positive to negative but was insignificant at $p < .05$. The fact that the sign on advertising tone changed is probably due to multicollinearity with the margin of victory variable.

26. First, I did this analysis subtracting the 1998 and 1992 rolloff rates. Because the mean values for rolloff were so much less in 1998 than in 1992, I next tried rank ordering the statewide results in each year. In both cases, the results were the same—no significant relationships were found.

27. Richard R. Lau, Lee Sigelman, Caroline Heldman, and Paul Babbitt, "The Effects of Negative Political Advertisements: A Meta-Analytic Assessment," *American Political Science Review* 93 (1999): 851–876.

28. It should be noted that all experimental studies do not find the same results as Ansolabehere and his colleagues. In particular, a recent experimental study by Joshua Clinton and John Lapinski finds no effect of negative ads on turnout. The Clinton and Lapinski study is superior to the work of Ansolabehere and his colleagues in two important ways: (1) it makes use of a national sample, as opposed to relying on subjects all from one geographic area; and (2) it has a sample size of over 10,000, more than three times larger than that obtained by the Ansolabehere team. See Joshua D. Clinton and John S. Lapinski, "An Experimental Study of Political Advertising Effects in the 2000 Presidential Race," paper prepared for the annual meeting of the American Political Science Association, 2001.

29. Ansolabehere and Iyengar, *Going Negative*, chap. 3.

30. For a graphical presentation of newspaper circulation rates since 1960, see George C. Edwards III, Martin P. Wattenberg, and Robert L. Lineberry, *Government in America*, 10th ed. (New York: Longman, 2002), p. 214.

8. How to Improve U.S. Turnout Rates

1. Malcolm Mackerras and Ian McAllister, "Compulsory Voting, Party Stability, and Electoral Advantage in Australia," *Electoral Studies* 18 (1999): 220.

2. Arend Lijphart, "Unequal Participation: Democracy's Unresolved Dilemma," *American Political Science Review* 91 (1997): 1–14.

3. Judge Griffin Bell, National Commission on Federal Election Reform, Public Hearing 1, Panel IV, transcript, p. 13.

4. Quoted in Lijphart, "Unequal Participation," p. 8.

5. See Megan Garvey and Mark Z. Barbak, "Cheney Admits to Sparse Texas Voting Record," *Los Angeles Times*, September 9, 2000, for the list of these sixteen elections.

6. American Political Science Association, "Toward a More Responsible Two-Party System: A Report of the Committee on Political Parties," *American Political Science Review* 44 (1950), supplement, number 3, part 2.

7. Ibid., p. 76.

8. See Martin P. Wattenberg, *The Decline of American Political Parties, 1952–1996* (Cambridge: Harvard University Press, 1998).

9. Anthony Corrado, "Elections in Cyberspace: Prospects and Problems," in *Elections in Cyberspace: Toward a New Era in American Politics,* ed. Anthony Corrado and Charles M. Firestone (Washington, D.C.: Aspen Institute, 1996), p. 29.

10. The exceptions were Delaware, Hawaii, and Louisiana, which held their primaries on Saturday, and Tennessee, which held its primary on Thursday.

11. Because the Jewish Sabbath ends at sundown, which would be fairly early in November, there would still be time for these people to vote. But clearly this would raise questions of fairness, and could lead to legal challenges.

12. Martin P. Wattenberg, "Should Election Day Be a Holiday?" *Atlantic Monthly,* October 1998, pp. 42–46.

13. Eric Lipton, "Problems Stir Calls to End '19th Century' Voting Process," *New York Times*, November 13, 2000.

14. President William Jefferson Clinton, "The Unfinished Work of Building One America," message to Congress, January 15, 2001.

15. In 2000, it was sadly ironic that on Tuesday, November 7th, many people did not have time in their busy day to vote, and less than a week later some of these same people were spending their Veterans' Day holiday at home glued to the continuous television coverage of the Florida recount.

16. CNN, "Carter: U.S. Voting Systems Unacceptable," posted at www.cnn.com on March 27, 2001.

17. National Commission on Federal Election Reform, "To Assure Price and Confidence in the Electoral Process," August 2001, p. 42.

18. Ruy A. Teixeira, *The Disappearing American Voter* (Washington, D.C.: Brookings Institution, 1992), p. 143.

19. R. Doug Lewis, "Fix the Vote, but Skip the Uniformity," *Washington Post*, December 24, 2000, p. B1.

20. "Wide Public Support Eludes LDP Candidates," *Asahi Shimbun*, July 15, 1998.
21. "Minshuto, Backed By Unaligned Voters, Rallied Late," *Asahi Shimbun*, July 1, 2000.
22. "A Halfhearted Push for Reform," *New York Times*, August 6, 2001.
23. Mackerras and McAllister, "Compulsory Voting," p. 233.

Index

Abramson, Paul, 34
All Saints Day, 169
American Political Science Association,
  164, 167
American Political Science Review (APSR),
  153, 155
American Voter, The (Campbell, Con-
  verse, Miller, and Stokes), 3, 9, 64
Ansolabehere, Stephen, 146, 149, 152,
  155–157, 159
Aristotle, Inc., 53
Arkansas, 14
Asahi Shimbun poll, 172–173
Australia: turnout in, 119; compulsory
  voting in, 164–166; voter friendly
  system in, 173
Australian Democrats, 19

Banfield, Edward, 22
Bartels, Larry, 155
Beck, Paul Allen, 25
Bell, Griffin, 165
Bennett, Stephen, 93
Bentham, Jeremy, 165
Berlusconi, Silvio, 23, 33
Black Republicans, 70
Blair, Tony, 33, 166
Blais, André, 77

Bloc Quebeçois, 33
Blondel, Jean, 18
Boyd, Richard, 37
Brady, Henry, 106
Brennan Center's "Buying Time" study,
  157
Brians, Craig, 118, 148, 156
Brody, Richard, 6
Budge, Ian, 144
Burnham, Walter Dean, 19, 25
Bush, George W., 5, 62, 107–110

Cable television, 91, 168
Caltech and MIT study, 9
Campaigns, presidential: 1840, 3;
  1948, 145; 1960 West Virginia pri-
  mary, 52
Campbell, Angus, 64, 112
Canada, registration in, 16–17
Candidate-centered politics, 2, 14, 21,
  32–34, 66, 162
Carmines, Edward, 31
Carter, Jimmy, 102, 171
Catch-all party, 23
Census Bureau studies, 38, 45, 68, 70,
  72, 79, 86, 95–96, 108
Chambers, William, 12
Cheney, Dick, 166